7.99

HOW TO
MAKE
MUSIC
IN YOUR BEDROOM
NICOLA SLADE

Virgin BOOKS

First published in Great Britain in 2007 by
Virgin Books Ltd
Thames Wharf Studios
Rainville Road
London
W6 9HA

A catalogue record for this book is available from the British Library.

ISBN 978-0-7535-1264-7

The paper used in this book is a natural, recyclable product made from wood grown
in sustainable forests. The manufacturing process conforms to the regulations of
the country of origin.

Typeset by Phoenix Photosetting, Chatham, Kent

Printed and bound in Great Britain by CPI Bookmarque Ltd, Croydon, CR0 4TD

1 3 5 7 9 10 8 6 4 2

CONTENTS

INTRODUCTION

There aren't many people out there who haven't picked up an instrument at some point in their lives, even if it was only at school. All the greats probably started out singing in the shower or the bath and there certainly aren't many of us who haven't dreamed of being a rock or pop star – the world's love of *Pop Idol* contests is testament to it. But sitting in the bath singing along to the radio, or applying to be on a reality TV show, as we have all seen, is not the best way to get your music heard.

It's becoming increasingly easy to make high-quality music without the need for a big studio or the funding of a record label. In the last few years many bands have embraced DIY methods to help promote and sell their music. Technology has taken the DIY ethic to a whole new level, allowing you to connect directly with the people who want to listen to, and hopefully buy, your songs.

Given that you don't want to try the reality TV route and might be put off by the thought of a record label executive making a quick buck out of the thing you are most proud of, you're going to need to get to grips with the basics of home recording.

After ten years spent kicking around venues, interviewing bands and industry types, and reporting on the music business itself, I came to realise that the fact that I didn't know how a song is made, from the initial creation of a melody through to producing and mastering, was plain embarrassing. I'd heard people chat about things like mixing, sequencers, Pro Tools and reverb, and while I enthusiastically nodded, I really had no idea what they were taking about. Meanwhile, I had started to share a flat with a singer-songwriter who is a DIY artist. I watched her mess about with vocal shields, tape duvets up against the walls and tinker with her Apple M-Powered home studio, and I became more and more intrigued.

The home computer, increased memory size, broadband and software applications have made home recording simple, opening doors for even the most inexperienced people. It's never been more exciting or fascinating – to be able to go online, scour the pages of MySpace, generate a playlist on Pandora, find a band in any country across the world and listen to something they have recorded themselves is a revolution in itself. Long gone are the days when you had to rely on your local record shop, a pirate radio station and the *NME* to discover something new, or feel frustrated that the only way to get your music heard was by signing on the line of a record label contract.

These recent developments don't mean that home recording and DIY haven't always existed. They have. Don't get too dizzied by the headlines saying that the Arctic Monkeys' game plan – to release early, home-recorded demos online for free to build a fanbase – was a true DIY masterstroke. Lots of hard work and the resources of a lot of people were involved in helping the band finally hit number one, including traditional backers such as a manager, a PR person, an agent and a record label. Same with Lily Allen – and she had the bonus of celebrity parentage.

DIY is where every song begins. The formation of a particular set of chords, a melody, a lyric, a bassline, a drum beat: they all start with someone, somewhere – maybe at home doing the washing up, or in their room ploughing through exam revision.

The DIY spirit is at the heart of popular music. Skiffle, a precursor to rock'n'roll popular in Britain in the 1950s, involved musicians using home-made or improvised instruments such as washboards, 'tea chest bass', kazoos, cigar-box fiddles, musical saws, and comb and paper. Its origins, in the US, stretch back to the 1920s in places such as Louisville, Kentucky and Memphis, Tennessee. Yet the music and its message spread – without the internet, mobile phones and email.

London and New York's punk and hip hop scenes were born of a similar DIY ethic. The three-chord rollicks of The Sex Pistols and The Clash and the parties led by Grandmaster Flash and Afrika Bambaataa were not the products of huge companies, given financial backing by media companies and sponsorship deals (although Malcom McLaren fancied himself something of a tycoon).

The dance music scene of the late 80s and early 90s in the UK and Europe was almost tribal in its growth and development. News spread via word of mouth to those in the know, and music created by DJs pounded out of speaker stacks at illegal raves in rural fields. You didn't see concert promoters supplying toilets and lighting rigs: it was all done by the DIY organisers.

Today, there's a whole host of bands and musicians utilising aspects of the DIY ethic – whether recording a song in a home studio or using the web to promote songs, or a combination of both. Some of the bands and artists profiled in this book have had what we might call recognisable success: musicians like Nizlopi, Grandaddy, The Crimea, Oisin and his father Donal Lunny and Jim Moray have had number one records, have sold hundreds of thousands of records, have even had record deals and opted to take the DIY approach instead. Some have diversified into DJing, producing, film soundtracks, advertising soundbeds and remixing. All make a living out of music using a DIY ethic. Meanwhile, some of the other guys profiled in this book are probably more like you, but have spent time building and learning how to use home studios – they're the guys who know all the tricks. Some work part-time, funding themselves to release music and get involved with musical projects. It's simple: there are no rules and there are many, many ways to get involved. Don't even be put off if you can't play anything – there are ways round that, as you will discover.

So, during a curious foray into my flatmate's home studio, I switched on the Mac, Pro Tools, the M Box and the microphone and created my version of Blondie's 'Union City Blues'. And, no, you can't find it on Bit Torrent sites – I might get in trouble for ignoring copyright issues. Jokes aside, recording music is simple once you've got a few basics under your belt. But finding out the basics is not so easy: people have many different ideas on how to approach home recording and it's easy to get lost in the geek-speak of it all.

Collected from hundreds of sources, this is a definitive, comprehensive round-up of the very basics. Let's go on the assumption you have a home computer, you know how to use it and somewhere you have a melody or lyric floating around your head. Let's also presume you're a bit like me: you've heard people chat about home recording, you can play a few chords and you like the idea of being a rock star. This could be the start of a long musical career.

Included is an overview of the equipment you'll require, how to set up a home studio in terms of the actual room you're using, what software applications can help you to record and edit music, and some of the technical bits and pieces such as mixing, mastering, effects and plug-ins. You'll also garner a few tips on how to get your music out there: how to promote and sell it without a record label.

The two most important things to remember at this stage are: don't be overwhelmed (if you can use a computer, you can get your head round this) and find a quiet place. The last thing you want is to annoy other people, or feel inhibited because someone might be listening in. Buy a load of blankets and duvets and some egg boxes. Clear out the mess in your bedroom/shed/garage/cupboard. Pad the room out a bit, load in your gear and get messing around.

Home recording and DIY has, for the first time, become a genuine threat to – or depending on how you look at it, an amazing opportunity for – the traditional music industry. Bands can record studio-quality music from their homes, package it up and sell it to fans online. It takes a lot of hard work and dedication, but it's not out of reach.

1
The basics

Your studio at home

Ever watched a documentary about your favourite band recording an album? More often than not they will be using a top-end studio: one that is expensive to build, maintain and use, with pricey engineers and beard-stroking producers. Sure, you can get an amazing sound from a professional studio, but they can be prohibitively expensive and intimidating spaces in which to record. And these days it's possible to create a near-professional quality recording environment in your own home and, with such great equipment out there at such reasonable prices, home recording is getting more popular all the time.

But a great studio isn't just about the equipment. Some recording studios are world-famous because of the actual 'space' itself – Phil Spector was a master of controlling space and used it to create his trademark 'Wall of Sound' noise. It's all in the acoustics of the room. Creating a great space is harder when you're setting up a studio in your bedroom, so what can you do to overcome this problem?

Nizlopi – Kieron Concannon, father of Luke Concannon, producer, manager, label boss of FDM Records

I spent the spring of 1997 in Marin County, California. Before I left the UK for this trip I was using an old

>>

Fostex 4-track cassette recorder and the very first Alesis Quadraveb which we used mostly on world music/Indo/ Celtic projects fusing sitars and uilleann pipes, Indian classical and film music etc. Whilst in America I had time to reflect on many bad experiences in studios in the UK. Most studios back then just weren't capable of recording real acoustic/ethnic instruments. If you didn't walk through the door with an electric guitar or keyboard they didn't have a clue. As I was using sitars, tablas and Irish bagpipes it was almost impossible to get good results. So I thought, 'Sod it, I'll build my own … in the back garden.'

Back in my 4-track days I had converted a spare bedroom into a very basic studio with minimal isolation from noise pollution. I put secondary double glazing on the window but still suffered from the bane of all home recording facilities, namely, low frequency rumble from the traffic outside – there was also a building site round the corner that didn't help. We used to set up duvets and blankets, whatever we could get our hands on, to surround the 'vocal booth' which was basically a few mic stands arranged around the vocalist to try and keep the outside-world bleed into the mic as low as possible.

Once back from the States, I signed up for a couple of music business and production courses in Nottingham and with the technical knowledge I gained from that I designed a studio we could build in the back garden. It was always going to be a shed but it had to be a sound-proof shed so it needed a lot of thought and a lot of concrete! Following a couple of acoustic projects with mainly folk artists, I produced Nizlopi's first-ever demo. Shortly after that we set up the label and recorded the first album, *Half These Songs Are About You,* which of course had 'JCB' on it, which went to number one in the UK in Christmas 2005.

Obviously we know that you guys have built a top-class studio set-up in your shed, but is it adequate enough for you to also mix and master?

Yes, we mix and occasionally master. For a commercial release we always use pro mastering. For demos, we use a pre-set from T Racks or a similar plug-in mastering tool, just to get the finished volumes closer to commercial levels. This is one area where home studios struggle – pro mastering can do so much to the finished levels and EQs, but is very expensive. Plug-ins go part of the way in giving home projects a chance at getting closer to those commercial levels; volume, apparently, is very important. Mixing is done on the Yamaha 02R, mastering either by a pro or with a plug-in.

What equipment do you use?

We started out with Logic Audio and an old beige Mac and a Yamaha 02R mixing desk. In its day the 02R brought so much flexibility and power to project studios, 40-plus ins and outs, digital effects and compressors on every channel – it was a terrific piece of kit. Last year we changed over to Pro Tools Lite and 002 rack mount unit. We also have a new Mac G5 computer … very powerful!

We have a couple of AKG 414s, probably one of the most adaptable condenser mics there has ever been. Back in the 4-track days we used budget dynamic mics made in Russia; they were very cheap but sounded great … just don't drop one on your toe!

How do you go about recording vocals?
The shed has a live room (separated from the control room with a double glazed patio door). In the bedroom days, we used to suspend duvets and blankets on mic stands surrounding the vocalist.

And drums/percussion?
One other issue for us is the need for Luke and John to 'perform' together whilst recording. We don't really adhere to the modern philosophy of 'tracking everything' (everything recorded separately) as we believe it's more important to capture the performance. With our shed, we don't have the space or facility to have complete audio separation whilst still maintaining eye contact between the two performers. The ideal situation would be to have two separate booths divided by a soundproof glass panel, then performers can see each other and hear each other – with headphones – but you get no 'spill' onto the mics from the other musician.

Do you use pre-recorded beats or samples?
Nizlopi projects hardly ever have what you would call 'samples'. John Parker supplies the beats with his

beat-boxing. Basically, we create everything ourselves. Nearly all our other projects will use samples at some stage of production as it makes life so much easier and it gives you a limitless palette of voices/colours. I think Luke and John are a bit perverse, really; it's a case of re-inventing the wheel on every project for them.

Any unusual techniques?

When recording the final track on *Half These Songs* (it's actually a 'ghost' track called 'Intro Song'), we put a microphone in the garden and made Luke sing it outside. If you listen closely you can hear the birds singing and some cars rumbling in the distance.

Any unconventional instruments?

We use a lot of unconventional instruments in all our projects. Here's a brief list:

- water harps – we designed and built these ourselves
- bul bul tarang, an Indian instrument resembling an accident between a typewriter and a lap steel guitar
- bowed bouzouki
- eik tara (one string banjo)
- bones
- brushed bodhrán
- harmonium

We have used a sample from Donald Rumsfeld and Tony Blair on the latest Nizlopi project.

Do you enjoy recording at home?

Having your own home facility gives you a greater degree of flexibility and can save you a ton of money; if the artist is having a bad day in a pro studio it can waste a lot of time and cost you a lot of money. With your own studio, if you're not feeling it you can switch the gear off and come back when you're in the mood and you haven't lost anything.

Does Nizlopi have a record/publishing deal?

We declined all major label offers for Nizlopi and set up our own label, FDM Records. We decided this was the best route for this band. We do have a publishing deal with Nuxx/Warner Chappell.

Any tips you'd pass on to others?

You can obtain great results with a home set-up if you are very careful and make some wise decisions on choice of gear. Too many home-based studios get seduced by the studio porn we see in all the studio magazines. What usually sets the pro studio apart from the home studio is the quality of the outboard gear, which is usually out of the range of the average bedroom studio. However, with careful mic placing and gain structure, the bedroom studio can capture some really great results. Many years ago, I was introduced to the following idea: wherever possible, buy a classic good-quality mic (or whatever piece of gear you need) and it will always be there for you. Better to have one or two pieces of really good gear than a studio full of cheap bits and pieces. For instance,

>>

> I would argue it would be better to get hold of a really good second-hand condenser mic (like a 414, for instance) and a good valve compressor. Get the microphone in the right place, really work on your gain structure and never ever adopt the idea that it can be fixed in the mix, and you won't go far wrong.

Selecting the ideal room

Your studio room needs to be as 'neutral' as possible. That means it should be as quiet as possible – keep furniture to a minimum so sounds don't bounce around, make sure the windows don't rattle, and if there is traffic noise, try to block it out. You need to be in a relatively empty and almost silent space to create a true, clean recording.

If you decide to 'mix' your records at home, then you don't want to be spending time editing out sounds you didn't even know you had recorded – the sound of a washing machine rumbling in the distance, or your family shouting on the phone. What's more, if sounds are bouncing off furniture and windows, these will likely be picked up by your sensitive recording equipment.

The ultimate goal is to minimise the reflection of the sound waves you produce as you play and record your music, and to prevent noise escaping the room. A room with carpet is your best bet, along with curtains, foam or blankets to line the walls and absorb sound. One DIY artist I met lined her bedroom walls with empty egg cartoons to absorb the noise from the outside world.

Make sure the people you live with (and your neighbours) aren't disturbed!

There is nothing worse than living with a musician who records the same song – and plays it back – over and over again. It is enough to drive anyone mad. Your recording may sound great to you, and you may feel truly inspired, but think how continual recording and playback sounds to others. To avoid trouble and test whether your recording room is adequately soundproof, play back at full volume something you've recorded and walk around your home to see what can be heard. If you can hear the music from the front door, then it's possible even the next door neighbours can hear it. If your home is surrounded by other people, or you live with friends and family, work on your recording at times when you are least likely to disturb others, and buy a decent pair of headphones.

What's the difference between traditional recording and modern home recording?

When you see professional studios with all of their desks, equipment, nuts, bolts, knobs, tapes and so on, it's easy to romanticise them and long to be in amongst all that exciting gear. And it is exciting. However, computers really can do the same job as professional studios these days and if you're on a tight budget then, ultimately, the choice is obvious.

There are some people who still choose to use old-fashioned equipment and some who prefer the modern, computerised path. Whatever you believe, the advantages of computer-based recording are hard to ignore, particularly for the home-based studio.

Firstly, it's quicker and easier to get to the finished product when you record with a computer, especially with additions such as CD burners and access to the internet. Another undeniable advantage of working on a computer with a program like Pro Tools or Cubase is the fact that you can get so much more for your money: more effects, more instruments, more tracks and higher-quality audio. Add to this the fact that you can constantly upgrade and update your studio whenever you need, and computer recording becomes an almost irresistible proposition.

Some would say that there are drawbacks: it's not always easy to learn how to use software programs (that's where this book comes in!), and some people say songs recorded in the old analogue style have more 'warmth' (go listen to some Beatles songs on vinyl and you'll see that this is often true). Some people simply like playing with old-fashioned equipment: the romance and nostalgia of it capture their imagination. Ditch it and come into the modern age!

Jason Lytle – Grandaddy

www.myspace.com/grandaddy

Grandaddy was formed in 1992 by singer/guitarist/keyboardist Jason Lytle, bassist Kevin Garcia and drummer Aaron Burtch. In 1995, guitarist Jim Fairchild and keyboardist Tim Dryden joined the band. Musically, the band features two guitars in the indie rock style, keyboards reminiscent of Philip Glass's minimalist style, and vocals in the key of Neil Young. The band's musical style combines experimental electronic sounds with elements of folk and rock.

Around the time the band's first album, *The Sophtware Slump*, was released, Grandaddy was invited to open for Elliott Smith on his tour for Figure 8. 'A.M. 180' from *Under the Western Freeway* was featured prominently during a sequence in the 2002 British film *28 Days Later*, and was also used as the title music for the BBC4 series *Charlie Brooker's Screenwipe*. Starting in late 2005, the Grandaddy song 'Nature Anthem' could be heard in a Honda Civic Hybrid television commercial, and it is currently heard in a Coca Cola commercial.

On 27 January 2006 Jason Lytle announced that the band had decided to split up. This was partially due to their work ethic in not releasing music on major labels or playing at typical Ticketmaster / Clear Channel-sponsored venues. The band has no plans to tour their final album, *Just Like the Fambly Cat*. Lytle intends to continue making music, and has recently embarked on a solo tour.

Have you recorded music at home?
My band and I have recorded four albums, in addition to a number of EPs and B-sides. All of these were made in a makeshift recording environment: garage, warehouse, storefront.

What kind of music do you make?
Grandaddy music was an ongoing attempt to make something grand sounding out of found scraps and ingenuity.

There was also a constant strive toward balance in sound – a clash of synthetic and organic in the hope that something original sounding would make it on to tape.

Do you mix and master your own records?
The last two albums were mixed in a dedicated mixing facility; everything else has been self-mixed. I always prefer to have someone else master the recordings.

What equipment do you use?
I have a Sony analog 24-track, an Otari ¼-inch 2-track and Pro Tools. I choose whichever medium will suit the music best. I have never been a purist or militant about recording. I have always simply read tips from my mentors and, more importantly, trust my ears and my feelings. My gear ranges from pretty good to awful and I use whatever is necessary to get the sound right.

How do you go about recording percussion?
I always have a room which is soundproofed or acoustically bland. I record the drums in there with as few microphones as possible and the drums played in a controlled manner. I will overdub cymbals and toms later if they are giving me too much hassle.

Do you use pre-recorded beats or samples?
I will use them occasionally if the song will benefit. I will do whatever to lift the song and make sure what I'm recording isn't played-out or boring.

How do you go about recording vocals?

I like to put a microphone at one end of the piano and record my vocals near the strings for a ghostly effect. I also like to record a drum set with one microphone and record the drum part twice, giving the drums a tight, double-tracked sound. Other than that I try to attempt new things, as I get bored very easily.

Have you used any sounds from the 'world around you' in your songs?

I have used baby chickens as a textural element in the breakdown of one of my songs called 'Jeez Louise'. I've used prescription painkillers in a shaker in a song about addiction. I even ran on a treadmill and miced it up for a good effect. My most recent favourite was probably my neighbour mowing his lawn, much to our frustration while we were trying to record the piano, until we realised that the mower was perfectly in tune with what we were recording. We recorded it quickly so we had it down before he finished.

Do you enjoy recording at home?

I only have limited experience of recording in proper studios, so 90 per cent of my recording is done in the screwed-up way that I've always done: by wearing yourself out and trying to get good sounds, and then rewarding yourself later by messing around with those sounds and having fun with it all.

>>

Do you think bands and artists can produce studio quality music at home?

Yes, it definitely is possible. I have had tremendous enjoyment hearing one of my recordings in a restaurant or shopping mall, knowing full well what the crude recording environment was, or knowing what colour my house slippers were when I tracked the tambourine.

Any tips?

Realise that home recording was primarily born from musicians craving more freedom. Don't be afraid to loosen up and have fun experimenting. Years down the road you will find yourself cherishing that stuff the most. Try and bypass the ears and get to the gut.

Basic equipment

Until recently, aspiring musicians interested in recording their original material had two options. The first was to invest in an array of often expensive equipment, usually including recording software or a multi-track recorder, cables, microphones, pre-amps and so on. The second option was to pay for time in a professional recording studio, an expense that can add up to thousands.

However, as more and more DJs, musicians and bands prove (including some of those featured in this book), it is now possible with a home computer to make a sound recording which is of good enough quality to be played on the radio and made available for purchase.

Even if your financial resources are limited, opportunities are available to jump-start your recording career by using cheap or even free technology. All it takes is your own creative spark, a little money, a computer and an internet connection.

This book points the way for artists, composers, DJs and musicians who would like to move their recording careers from ground zero. The advice in this guide is based upon experience with certain kinds of equipment and software. It does not represent the final word in home recording – that is a massive subject which you could research for the rest of your life. The earth shall be inherited by the geeks, after all.

The basic hardware and software necessities

Assuming you have instruments already and you've cleared out your cupboard, shed, bedroom or garage, you're going to need a computer. If you're using a PC, you'll need to check it has the following:

1. Microsoft Windows 98 SE or later. It is increasingly the case that newer software packages are compatible only with later versions of Windows. Be sure to check the minimum requirements listed on the software of your choice.
2. A processor of 400 MHz (Pentium III minimum).
3. At least 10 GB of free hard disk space.
4. At least 256 MB of RAM to run the software.
5. A Windows-compatible sound card.

You will need to have these basics in order to run recording software applications and sequencers, plus enough capacity to edit, add effects, save and store.

If you have an Apple Mac, you will find that the most recent versions actually include some kind of sound editor. However, to record music properly, you will have to buy Mac or Mac-friendly software such as Pro Tools.

Digital audio interfaces and sound cards

A sound card or digital audio interface is absolutely essential if you are a musician recording your own electronically generated music. This card or 'box' will act as the interface between your computer and your outboard gear – you simply plug your gear into the card or 'box', which is in turn connected to your computer.

Outboard gear is electronic equipment such as signal processors, microphones and any other electronic components that are not internal to your computer and/or part of your recording software. In order to get your electronic instruments or your outboard gear connected to and communicating with your computer, you are going to need a sound card or a recording interface. Using a sound card is the cheapest and simplest option, but audio interfaces expand your options and improve quality.

If you are a DJ working with pre-recorded loops, you will also need a sound card to play back your music, although this won't always be necessary for recording music that you are playing on your non-electronic, non-MIDI instruments. An exception to this rule is of course if you are generating beats or sounds using a keyboard or any other kind of outboard MIDI-based equipment (for more on MIDI-based equipment see pages 39–40)

Basic sound cards come with two ports into which you can plug a microphone or other equipment. One is a ⅛-inch port (otherwise known as a 'jack') that is specifically for your microphone. The second port is called the line input port, into which you can plug other equipment. If you have the cash, it is well worth investing in a high-end sound card to achieve better results.

That is your simplest option. However, as technology has advanced, there are a number of other options available to you, namely digital audio interfaces made by companies such as M-Audio and Lexicon. Quite often you will be able to purchase the interface between your instruments and your computer with built-in recording software in a bundle, effectively creating a ready-made digital audio workstation (see page 38).

A good example of a basic sound card (available for roughly £50) is the M-Audio Audiophile 2496. It gives you two analogue line ins, for microphones or other equipment, and two outs on RCA jacks (the cable connection) plus a total of four digital (S/PPIF – a proprietary digital format) ins and four outs of high-quality input/ouput (I/O). The card (actually, it's more of a small box) is compatible with Mac and PC.

The company also makes another sound card called the Delta 1010 LT PCI (roughly £100), which allows you to plug in your outboard gear and instruments as well as boasting zero latency (delay).

There are many companies producing sound cards. You might also want to take a look at Realtek and Creative Labs or check websites like Sound On Sound or Amazon for more details.

Your other option is to purchase a complete box, which, as mentioned previously, might include some bundled recording software application. Later we'll look at M-Powered Pro Tools, which requires you to purchase the Digidesign M-Audio box – the preferred choice for lots of musicians.

Examples of complete boxes – which contain almost everything to get you off the ground – include the Lexicon Alpha, Omega and Lambda USB Audio Interfaces, which come with Cubase software, or the range of Digidesign M Boxes. All of them offer USB/FireWire connection to your computer, multiple inputs – sometimes up to ten channels of analogue – for your instruments and headphone outputs for almost all different types of headphones. Some of them will even include extra plug-ins (see chapter 3 for more on plug-ins). Boxes can cost from £100 upwards. It's best to check online for more details and pricing.

Ben Morgan

Ben started playing guitar at sixteen. 'To stave off boredom', he began recording songs on a double tape deck with a built-in mic and managed to use that as a crude recording device for several months. When Christmas came along, he pooled his money to buy a second-hand Tascam 4-track tape recorder, while managing to get his hands on a couple of old dynamic microphones and hooked up his Commodore Amiga to provide drum sounds.

A few years later, after two aborted non-musical degrees, Ben started an HND Sound Engineering. Several years on, he uses a PC-based home recording set-up, making tracks that have been used in shows broadcast by the American network NBC.

Do you record music at home?
On the whole I try to produce the finished product at home.

>>

>>

Can you explain what kind of music you make?
At the moment I'm mostly making acoustic music, although in the past I have also produced dance music in my home studio.

What equipment/software do you use to record music at home?
Hardware:
- microphones (Shure SM57, AT4047, AT4050, 2xOktava Mk-012)
- small mixing desk (Spirit Folio SX)
- 2 x DI boxes
- Tannoy Reveal loudspeakers
- headphones & headphone amplifier
- MIDI controller keyboard – Studiologic SL-990XP
- RealTraps Portable Vocal Booth
- Echo Mia sound card

Software:
- Cubase SX3
- various plug-ins

How do you go about recording vocals at home?
I have a corner of the room set up for recording vocals and acoustic instruments/percussion. I have acoustic foam stuck to two office partition boards with spray adhesive and these are put behind the vocalist (who is facing into the room) to deaden the sound bouncing back into the mic. I also use the RealTraps Portable Vocal Booth behind

>>

the microphone to further deaden the sound of the room and prevent some of the original signal hitting reflective surfaces etc.

How do you go about recording instruments/percussion at home?

I record acoustic instruments in the same way as the vocals outlined above. For electric guitar and bass guitar, I plug into a DI box and then record into the computer direct. I can then play with the raw signal using guitar amp emulation software plug-ins. I used to record electric guitar by putting a mic in front of the amp but I do this less and less these days (also my amp is broken!).

I also rely on 'virtual instruments' for piano/organ/orchestral sounds — these are played in via the MIDI controller keyboard.

Do you use samples, or pre-recorded beats?

Sometimes I use drum loops, other times I will program in drum loops using individual drum 'hits' in the MIDI drum editor. For some material I record a drummer at a local studio and bring the drum parts back home to work with.

Do you use any unconventional instruments, or take samples from 'the world around you' to use in your music? If so, please explain.

I occasionally use glockenspiel and kazoo and have just purchased a melodica, but nothing more unusual than that.

Do you mix and master your own records?

Yes, always. Mixing takes place completely inside Cubase SX3; no outboard is used at all. I master in an audio editor such as Wavelab using plug-ins.

Do you enjoy recording at home?

Fifty/fifty. I enjoy the fact that you can work at your own pace and that you can break to watch TV or get something to eat or drink etc. Also the obvious financial benefits make it more attractive to most people.

However there are a plethora of negatives in my opinion:

- Home studios are not always the most conducive to creativity.
- Equipment is usually of a poorer standard/quality than in a commercial studio, and if anything breaks down you don't have someone on site to repair it or hire another one in.
- Acoustic conditions are at best mediocre in most home studios.
- If you are a musician then you should be focusing solely on your performance and not worrying about all of the technical considerations that were traditionally within the domain of the engineer.

Do you think musicians/producers can generate album-quality material at home, or is it better to use a studio?

Yes, but equally you could produce a terrible-sounding album at Abbey Road studios. If the musician/producer is capable then you can get great results out of very modest equipment. If the musician/producer is incompetent it doesn't matter where the album is made or with what equipment — it all comes down to the capabilities of the individual(s) in my opinion.

Do you have a record/publishing deal? If so, who with?
No, although we have a licensing deal with a company in America who place our music in TV and film in the States. The company are called Rescue Records.

Can you give one or two recommendations to other people who are getting into recording music at home?
I believe the most important thing is to read up on several key subjects:

- microphone placement and choice
- gain structure
- basic room acoustics and loudspeaker positioning
- use of effects and processors

Immerse yourself in recording culture, subscribe to a recording magazine, visit lots of recording websites/forums etc. By deciding to record at home you are wearing many hats at once: producer, engineer, assistant engineer, runner, maintenance engineer, tea-boy etc. These are all skilled positions so it is imperative to try to think like they would rather than just thinking like a musician or a DJ.

Also purchase wisely. It is often better to have one or two decent pieces of equipment which will last years and sound good rather than lots of cheap equipment which will either break or malfunction quickly.

Don't forget room acoustics. At present this is a hot topic and rightly so – if you can't hear accurately in the room then you instantly are at a disadvantage. There are many inexpensive options available, both DIY and ready-made. Although sound absorption materials are not as sexy as a new guitar or microphone, they can have a much bigger influence on your sound.

Microphones

The best piece of advice any home recording artist can get is to buy a good microphone. Without one you won't be able to record anything – instruments or vocals – effectively. Most home computers today come with a small microphone, but it's no good relying on this: the sound will always be atrocious. But don't be alarmed – there are plenty of cheap mics out there that will do the job.

Check out the websites www.musciansfriend.com and www.zzounds.com for more information – they are both a fantastic resource.

Before you buy, it's a good idea to learn about the different types of microphones, so that you can choose the right one for your needs.

Types of microphone

When selecting microphones to use either live or in your home studio, you'll come across two different varieties: dynamic and condenser. Let's take a look at both of these microphone types, and their advantages and disadvantages.

Condenser Microphones

Condenser microphones are most frequently found in recording studios because of their ability to pick up a great range of sound frequencies and their 'transient response', which means how effectively they reproduce the 'speed' of an instrument or voice.

Condenser microphones are more expensive and more fragile than dynamic microphones. They also require the use of a power supply, generally 48 volt 'phantom power' (see page 155 for more on phantom power) and are generally used only in studios because of their sensitivity to loud sounds.

With condenser microphones, you'll generally find two different sub-types: small diaphragm and large diaphragm. The diaphragm is, in a very basic sense, the fabric which captures your sound.

Large diaphragm microphones (LDMs) are used to record studio vocals and any instrument where a more thorough sound is desired. This is because large diaphragm mics are particularly senstive. They are generally used to pick up one specific noise at a time.

Small diaphragm microphones (SDMs) are generally the best choice when you are recording a number of instruments at one time in the same room because, despite the fact they are smaller, they pick up a wide range of frequencies. Often you will need more than one positioned around the room to record all of your instruments effectively.

Among some of the condenser microphones namechecked by musicians are the Oktava MC012, RODE NT1 and AKG C414B and also those made by the company Shure.

Dynamic Microphones

Compared to condenser microphones, dynamic microphones are much tougher and, since they are resistant to water, are good for use outdoors or onstage. The Shure SM57 and Shure SM58 are famous for not just their great sound quality, but also the fact you can chuck them about without breaking them – ideal for rock and punk bands who like to let things go a bit!

Dynamic microphones don't require their own power supply like condenser microphones, so you can plug them into a computer or an amp and they will work straight away, without an independent power supply.

Watch out if you record using a dynamic mic, as they are nowhere near as accurate as condenser mics. But if you want to capture loud guitars, live vocals and drums, then you will definitely need one.

Among those named by the musicians in this book are Shure SM57 and Shure SM58, and Sennheiser E602.

Choosing the right microphone

To record vocals at home, it's best to get a large-diaphragm dynamic microphone.

To record acoustic guitar, a good small-diaphragm condenser microphone will suffice.

To record strings, a large-diaphragm condenser microphone is ideal because, while the strings resonate quickly, the 'slower transient response' of the large-diaphragm microphone will record the sound in its true state.

If you are a drummer, then you'll need a combination of dynamic and condenser microphones. Put a dynamic mic on the drums themselves and then for cymbals, you'll want small diaphragm condenser microphones, as they give the best frequency and transient response.

Cables

Generally speaking, most professional microphones use what is called a three-pin XLR cable. XLR cables come in two styles, those with three-pin attachments on either end and those with a three-pin attachment at one end and a stereo ¼-inch plug at the other end.

If you have a high-end sound card you should be able to plug in the ¼-inch cable directly. If you have an ordinary sound card you'll need an adapter that reduces the size of the plug from stereo ¼-inch to stereo ⅛-inch.

Most XLR cables are relatively inexpensive and easy to find on the net. One additional comment about cables should be made here: **you do not have to use a mic to record your instrument**. If your instrument has a pick-up, you can plug the ¼-inch instrument cable into your sound card and directly record what you are playing. Standard instrument cables have stereo ¼-inch plugs on either end so you will need to buy the appropriate instrument cable to plug into your instrument and then into the computer. These cables generally cost between £5 and £20, depending on the quality of the cable.

Thurston Revival

A Canadian singer-songwriter who releases material in his own country through the Dark Arts Gramophone Company. He has caught the eye of the London-based music industry and is set to release a single through Record of the Day in summer 2007.

Do you record music at home?
Yes, all of it.

Do you mix and master your own records?
Mastering should never be done by the same person that mixed the music. They are separate crafts that very few people are any good at. Home mixing is killing music!

What equipment/software do you use to record music at home?
- Pro Tools Digi 002
- Avalon 737 pre-amp/compressor
- G4 laptop
- Shure SM7 mic
- Neumann U67 mic
- Beyer ribbon mic
- Drawmer de-esser

How do you go about recording vocals at home?
It is crucial to remember that you are an artist, not a computer programmer. Set up a system that you could

use if you were blind drunk. Then I recommend getting blind drunk. Find a mic, cheap or dear, that flatters your vocal.

Can you explain any unusual recording techniques you have used to capture a particular sound?
I mounted some guitar pickups inside my old battle-worn upright piano, fed the signals into a cranked-up Marshall on the other side of the room and adjusted the volume so it was on the threshold of feeding back. Depressing the piano's sustain pedal changes the harmonic content of the sound – every time I would push down the pedal, the chords would slowly morph into otherworldly feedback.

Do you enjoy recording at home?
Yes. Most studios are as inspiring as a dentist's office.

Do you think musicians/producers can generate album-quality material at home, or is it better to use a studio?
Joe Meek recorded 'Telstar' in his flat. Enough said.

All you need is a single signal path that sounds amazing. Just one. Avoid running through a mixer before tape unless it is amazing. Forget about tracking stereo – it's over-rated. In the studio, when the clock is ticking by at a couple hundred quid per hour, most people play far too safe, avoid experimenting, and don't indulge in the source of most great things – pointless messing about. There are some things that are best done in a studio – some things just need a great sounding room. Most studio owners are losing their shirts and will be happy to give you a deal to fill their downtime. Obsolete recording gear goes cheaply – 24-bit digital decks, analogue 8 tracks, last year's fashionable outboard pre-amp and so on.

Can you give one or two recommendations to other people who are getting into recording music at home?
The very first thing: do not proceed until you have clean AC power! If every time your sister turns on the hair-dryer you hear it on your tracks, if your neighbours' fluorescent lights cause buzzing, sort it out before everything else. Unless your room sounds great, deaden it up. Most rooms suffer from unflattering pings and reflections. Clap your hands a few times and you'll know. Things like blankets and carpet only take out some high frequency reflections. Packing blankets and mattresses work quite well. Extraneous noise *must* be eliminated if you are micing anything quieter than blazing amp ... the clanking of cutlery, the number 9 bus going by outside, the cranky old lady downstairs banging on her ceiling with a broom. Whenever possible use a high end A/D converter as a clock source instead of your computer. The improvement is substantial.

A favourite recording anecdote?
Most of my vocals are tracked inside The Monolith, an airtight semi-soundproof five-mattress fort. It gives me

>>

a strong incentive to nail the take first time – within ten minutes most of the oxygen is used up and with the added heat from tube outboard gear, the temperature in the monolith becomes extreme. I've only fainted from hypoxia once.

2
Your digital audio workstation

Turning your computer into a home recording studio

Now that we've covered some of the basics, you'll need to get to grips with turning your home computer into a digital audio workstation. The digital audio workstation is central to your being able to record, edit and save your music at a relatively low cost. A typical digital audio workstation combines a multitrack audio recorder with audio editing software.

In this chapter, we look into equipment and software applications that allow you to record your instruments and vocals into your home computer, and even allow you to add effects, arrange and create songs without the need of actual instruments at all.

If you are looking to digitally record your guitars, drums, keyboards and vocals at home, then you'll need to create a complete digital audio workstation. Musicians also use software known as sequencers to edit and arrange songs separately, and so these are usually a part of modern digital audio workstations. There are a vast number of sequencer applications available, but to get you off the ground, we'll describe the much-lauded Pro Tools, Logic, FL Studio (Fruity Loops), Propellerhead Reason, Cubase, Sony SoundForge, Audacity and GarageBand. A web search for 'music recording software' will present you with a million more results, but these applications provide a decent starting point.

It's important to bear in mind that these pieces of kit can achieve enormous amounts, so much so that you can spend years learning how to perfect using them. There are thousands of tutorials on the web and even colleges which teach budding and experienced musicians/engineers/producers how to use these tools.

Here we will show how these software programs differ, give you an understanding of their basic functions — occasionally going into more depth for those of you who might have downloaded free trials — and explain what kind of computer you will need to get the application running, as well as other useful hints and tips (for example, how much they cost and whether you can get them for free!).

Before we get started though, it's a good idea to learn the basics about sequencers.

What is a sequencer?

A sequencer is a computerised machine that 'plays' musical performances. Using the industry-standard computer language MIDI, which allows electronic musical equipment and computers to communicate with each other, the sequencer tells equipment that can make musical sounds (for example, a keyboard) what musical notes to play, and when to play them. If you are into web design, a comparison can be drawn with HTML — the code tells the internet what to display and where — it's exactly the same principle. A MIDI message is produced by your electronic instrument and can then be recorded or played back by your computer.

An example of a very simple sequencer is Windows Media Player. This software does not have any facility to record MIDI messages, nor edit them. It can only playback a MIDI performance (stored in MIDI File Format). Such simple playback-only sequencers are often called 'MIDI Players'.

Because MIDI controls electronic-only instruments, and can't record the sound of acoustic instruments or human voice, digital audio recording and playback is a feature that is often added to sequencers. The sequencer will playback tracks of digital audio in sync with the MIDI tracks.

Recording a musical performance using MIDI

Most sequencers allow you to record your song directly into them (and therefore, straight to your computer's hard drive) just as though they were recording a performance on an old-style cassette tape.

Sequencers save recordings in their own language – MIDI messages in MIDI File Format data files, and when they are prompted, they will playback your material as actual sounds. Don't worry – you won't be hearing a series of random computer bleeps!

The sequencer also keeps track of the pace of your songs during the recording so that it can record the 'rhythm' of your instruments. A sequencer might also have the facility to make a metronome sound which acts as a guide during recording, so that you can keep the same rhythm when recording different tracks.

Playing a musical performance using MIDI

When a sequencer plays back your recording, it mimics the exact process you went through to create a particular sound. The sequencer does this by sending the MIDI messages that the musical instrument generated when you played it (and which you recorded using your sequencer) *back* to the instrument, like a mirror. So, if you hit middle C on the keyboard, the sequencer will play back middle C. It will fully duplicate your performance.

Advantages of sequencers

Sequencers allow you to easily edit your recordings and scrub out any mistakes you've made along the way. This is infinitely easier than trying to correct mistakes recorded onto magnetic tape, or even digital audio recorders, which is why musicians use sequencers so much nowadays.

Most sequencers offer the facility to enter notes (and other control data such as volume/pan/vibrato and so on) by 'step-entering' the data. You don't have to play the musical part in real-time. Instead, you can slowly enter each musical note (and other effects), and specify the musical bar and beat upon which it is to be played.

Most sequencers also have very intuitive interfaces. For example, many allow you to step-enter notes by clicking the mouse pointer upon a graphical sheet of music manuscript drawn upon the screen. Digital audio recorders do not typically have such features. With digital audio recorders, you are only able to record actual instruments directly onto your computer (something you can't do using MIDI), and so digital recording capacity is usually included in sequencer software in addition to all the other features.

Computers as sequencers

Most computers these days will have enough capacity to carry a sequencer. They either can be purchased off the shelf in packs or are available – sometimes free – as downloads from the web. With a sound card installed in your computer, the sequencer can play back musical performances without even needing external MIDI hardware such as Audacity and Cubase.

Examples of sequencers

- Ableton Live
- Acid and Cinescore from Sony
- Cubase and Nuendo from Steinberg
- Digital Performer and AudioDesk from MOTU
- FL Studio from Image Line Software
- Live from Ableton
- Logic Pro, Logic Express and GarageBand from Apple
- Pro Tools from Digidesign
- Reason from Propellerhead
- Samplitude, Sequoia, Music Maker and Music Studio from Magix
- SAWStudio from RML Labs
- Sonar, Project5 and Home Studio from Cakewalk
- Storm from Arturia
- Tracktion from Mackie

In the following pages you will learn about some of these sequencers and home recording software applications.

Alastair Brown

After studying music in Chichester, West Sussex, in 2000 Alastair 'left for the big lights, bright city of London town and the seductive lure of the music industry'. After completing a work experience placement, Alastair worked for three years to become head of music at the radio company Student Broadcast Network (SBN). Alastair's first love, playing and recording music, has never gone away. After a recent rediscovery of traditional (and not so traditional) folk music, he has teamed up with Radio 2 Folk Award nominee Lauren McCormick (The Devil's Interval) to write and record material.

Do you record music at home?
Yes, I record at home and have done for a couple of years. They're mostly demo recordings that I use to get gigs, sell at shows and send off to publishers. It's also very useful as a solo writer/performer to have these recordings to listen back to in order to make improvements to the songs.

Can you explain what kind of music you make?
I'm a solo acoustic singer-songwriter. It's just me and an acoustic guitar, so on that level the music I record is very simple. However, I try to use strong melody, catchy guitar parts, interesting lyrics and unusual song structures to lend the songs their sophistication. All music rubs off in one way or another but I'm currently particularly influenced by the US alt. country scene and UK folk roots music.

Do you mix and master your own records?
Of course! For me this is an important part of the home recording experience/procedure.

What equipment/software do you use to record music at home?
This is the full monty:

>>

Recording:
- DPA 4090 condenser microphone
- 2 x Røde K2 valve mic (DPA & K2 for guitar, K2 for vocals)
- SPL Gold Mike 9844 tube pre-amp
- Joe Meek VC7 pre-amp
- Mackie 1604-VLZ Pro (16-track mixing desk)
- Alesis ADAT HD24 (24-track multi-track recorder)

Playback:
- Marantz Amp PM-66SE
- Tannoy speakers

Mixdown/Master:
- Mackie 1604-VLZ Pro (16-track mixing desk)
- Focusrite Platinum Mix Master (compression & EQ)
- Focusrite Platinum Penta (compression)
- Behringer SNR 2000 (denoiser)
- SPL 9629 (de-esser)
- Tascam CD-RW900

Duplication:
- Alesis CD Twin

How do you go about recording vocals at home?
I use a very good quality valve microphone (RØDE K2) going through an equally good pre-amp (SPL Gold Mike 9844). This maximises the sound quality and warmth of the vocal. I always use a pop shield and have a very close mic technique to achieve an intimacy with the voice. If I'm recording 'as live' (recording vocal and guitar

>>

>>

simultaneously) I try and create maximum separation of vocal and guitar by using foam behind and below the vocal mic. Isolating the vocal this way allows much greater control for mixing levels afterwards. The pre-amp output goes directly into the multi-track recorder (Alesis ADAT HD24), which records the sound.

How do you go about recording instruments/percussion at home?

The instrument I record mostly is acoustic guitar. For this I use two microphones in order to create a stereo recording and thus a fuller sound. The DPA 4090 is placed very close to the guitar just about where the fretboard joins the body of the instrument. The other mic (RØDE K2) is slightly further away and positioned below the body of the guitar facing up, just away from the sound hole. Both microphones are used to complement one another and, as with vocals, I make sure these go through good valve pre-amps to give the warmest natural tone. Again, the pre-amp outputs go directly into the multi-track recorder.

How do you mix and master your own records?

Generally I'll be mixing down just three separate tracks (one vocal and the two guitar tracks). The vocal and guitar outputs from the ADAT recorder go through a compressor and EQ and I may use the de-esser on the vocal (it does what it says on the tin – reduces the harsh hiss of a sung 'sss' sound). Each track then goes through the mixer where they're panned left or right (centre for the vocal)

>>

>>

and master volume is set before it's all recorded down onto CDR. I'll listen closely back to the first mix, probably make a few adjustments and continue the process until I have a final mix I'm happy with. This usually takes four or five attempts. I always make a note of the settings so if, after a few more listens, I'm not satisfied, I can go back and remix again without starting from scratch.

Can you explain any unusual recording techniques you have used to capture a particular sound?
Recording in a bathroom or tiled shower room can create a wonderful reverb vocal sound (why else is singing in the shower so popular?). Make sure there's no chance of getting wet, though, otherwise at best your mic will be ruined, at worst you'll be dead.

Do you enjoy recording at home? If so, what's so special about it?
Yes. I love being able to record at any time, day or night (assuming no one else is in the house). It means that when inspiration strikes I'm ready and there's none of the pressure associated with studio recording (time, cost, a less than enthusiastic engineer, etc.). This affords the chance to experiment more and there's the whole satis-faction of knowing I've done it all myself. Plus, most importantly, I can record nude.

Do you think musicians/producers can generate album-quality material at home, or is it better to use a studio?
Well, first define 'album quality'. Some albums sound

amazing with a rough and ready lo-fi approach and if they were given the full production treatment would lose their appeal. Certainly more ambitious projects need a lot of care to avoid sounding too homemade, but it can be done. I think the key point is that with the absence of studio pressures (see the previous question) musicians are free to perform in a relaxed environment, so home recording can capture them at their best and most natural.

Can you give one or two recommendations to other people who are getting into recording music at home?
It sounds obvious, but find somewhere quiet. It's surprising what some microphones can pick up. You can insulate a room with all kinds of padding (hang up some duvets, sleeping bags, blankets, whatever really) but be careful not to make the room sound too 'boxy'.

Also, experiment with microphone positions. It may take a while to find the optimum positions for your particular set-up.

Can you give me your favourite recording anecdote?
Not an anecdote as such, but an example of how sensitive microphones can be. Having asked everyone in the house to be quiet, I remember getting angry with my brother for stirring his tea too loudly – the mic was picking that up from two rooms away. I realised then that to avoid any family breakdowns it would be best to record only when the house is empty.

GarageBand

GarageBand is probably one of the simplest tools for recording music and provides a brilliant starting point for beginners. The software is owned by Apple and comes installed on all new Apple Macs. Assuming you are a beginner and mostly work on Macs, it might be wise to figure out this program first before attempting something more sophisticated such as Pro Tools or Logic.

Because it's so simple, it's best to make it our first software overview. The stuff that you learn here will provide you with a basic sense of what all software packages can accomplish.

Bear in mind that GarageBand is only available as a part of iLife, a suite of applications (also including iPhoto, iMovie, iDVD, iTunes and iWeb) created by Apple Mac. iLife is included on new Macintosh computers and upgrades can be purchased separately.

The software is based on loop-based music sequencing software which first appeared in the late 1990s. The application comes with more than a thousand pre-recorded sampled and sequenced loops, and fifty samples, which can be played using a MIDI keyboard connected to the computer. Additional loops and instruments are available in the five GarageBand Jam Packs, separate products offered by Apple Computer; each expansion pack costs approximately £50–60 and adds more than two thousand loops and dozens of virtual instruments.

Who uses GarageBand?

Nine Inch Nails frontman Trent Reznor released singles in 2005 called 'The Hand That Feeds' and 'Only' as GarageBand files, allowing people to freely remix them. The first single from their

2007 album *Year Zero*, called 'Survivalism', has also now been released in this way, as well as a host of other tracks.

Jay-Z, Limp Bizkit and even Mike Oldfield have referred to GarageBand as one of their favourite recording tools.

Key features

So, what can GarageBand do? Here is a brief summary of some of its highlights.

● First up, if you are in a band, or record as solo artist, you still have provision to record up to eight real instruments and one software 'instrument' at the same time, providing you have an appropriate audio interface connected to your computer (see page 22 for more on digital audio interfaces). Be careful with using all eight tracks however. It is possible that your computer won't have enough memory and while recording you might find that a couple of tracks drop out or disappear. Sometimes it's wise to buy an external memory drive to store your songs.

● You can import MIDI, Apple AAC and Sony ACID music files into GarageBand to mess about with. MIDI files are imported as 'software instrument regions', Apple AAC files are imported as 'real instrument regions', and ACID files are imported as 'real instrument loops'.

● Making loops is particularly easy with GarageBand's Apple Loops feature, allowing you to record and edit your own music, or pilfer the Apple Loops library for pieces of music you want to use.

● GarageBand's Musical Typing turns your computer keyboard into a music keyboard so that you can play and record software instruments. You can control what octave you play in, and control velocity and other controller information (including mod wheel, pitch bend and sustain) of the notes you play.

- You can transpose (change the pitch of) a song to a different key, to add interest and variety to your songs. When you transpose a song using the master pitch curve, real and software instrument regions (both your recordings and loops) are transposed to the new key.

- You can check and enhance the tuning of real instrument tracks that have the right rhythmic feel but are not perfectly in tune, using the Enhance Tuning slider, located in the real instrument editor. You can also enhance the timing of real instrument tracks which contain the right notes but are not perfectly in time, again using the Enhance Timing slider.

- The latest version of GarageBand features a wealth of new software instruments, including two new synthesisers, Hybrid Basic and Hybrid Morph. You can use these synthesisers, which are based on waveforms, to create rich, complex sounds. It also features new effects, including a gender-shifting voice effect (is that the trick Cher uses?), new guitar amp simulations and bass amp simulations.

Lisa Knapp

Lisa Knapp has emerged as a highly distinctive artist on the alternative folk scene. She merges a style of traditional folk and self-penned songs, with violin, hammer dulcimer and banjo. She released her debut album, *Wild*

>>

and Undaunted, on her own Ear to the Ground Records (distributed by Pinnacle) in March 2007. Tracks from *Wild and Undaunted* have been played on BBC Radio 1, 2, 3, 6 Music, Radio Scotland and Radio Wales as well as several local stations across the UK. To date Lisa has done live sessions/interviews for the Huw Stephens show (Radio 1), the Mike Harding show (Radio 2), the Andy Kershaw show (Radio 3) and Stuart Maconie's Freak Zone (6 Music). She is co-produced by her partner, Gerry Diver.

Do you record music at home/ have you ever recorded music at home?

Lisa: Yes, I have recorded at home. For *Wild and Undaunted*, I worked very closely with Gerry and we recorded everything ourselves. Some tracks were literally done in my front room; most were done in our studio. As this is my first album, I am relatively new to the whole process of recording, which is a real hidden art. Gerry is much more experienced at recording and his years of experience were invaluable, especially with regard to the technical side of things.

Gerry: 'Blacksmith' was recorded in our bedroom and was later remixed by Youth. 'Lavender' was recorded by Lisa at home in the front room and mixed in a studio.

Can you explain what kind of music you make?

For this album I worked mainly with traditional English folk songs but also some original work, some collaborative, some my own.

>>

Do you mix and master your own records?

Gerry: The album was mixed by Chris Brown, a very experienced engineer who used to be senior engineer at Abbey Road. He mixed it at his own studio but it was still mixed 'in the box' completely, using Logic Pro and a few third-party plug-ins: PSP vintage warmer, Altiverb and so forth. I wanted a fresh pair of ears and there was a deadline looming so having Chris was great in terms of getting things finished on time.

For the singles that are not on the album, I mixed them myself in our own studio. Mastering was done by Donal Whelan at Hafod Mastering. With the wonders of broadband it's all done via the internet. This entails Donal downloading the finished mixes from our iDisk server and uploading the mastered version back up there when he's done.

What equipment/software do you use to record music at home?

Gerry: Sony c48 mics and Neumann mics into a TL audio pre-amp (Ivory series) going into an m-audio sound card using a Mac running Logic 7 ... although Lisa sometimes records into GarageBand which opens up beautifully into Logic Pro for editing and mixing.

Lisa: I really rate GarageBand for sheer plug-in-and-go-ness, which is really good for catching ideas in the moment. It's great for doodling and getting basic tracks up to a certain point, especially with some of the tracks

>>

which were just one vocal and one instrument. You can then open up into Logic and take it further.

How do you go about recording vocals at home?

Lisa: We experimented with various mic positions and used close micing on a few occasions, testing out different areas in the room and so on.

Gerry: Using a great condenser mic (cardioid) in our front room. I'd prefer to use the bedroom, but that's not always possible, due to our daughter sleeping in the next room. Bedrooms are so dead acoustically and are ideal for recording vocals as there are usually so few reflections.

When recording in our living room we sometimes hang up duvets to deaden things a bit although if things are close miced you can get pretty respectable results. The only downside with close micing, I find with the mic on cardioid setting that the proximity effect can be a bit much. For 'George Collins' I recorded Lisa playing live on guitar and voice in our living room and then brought the track into our proper studio to add piano, mandolin and bass and to mix it. I find this to be quite a natural approach for capturing a mood. Most performers play at their most relaxed at home and if you capture a really sparkling vocal performance then the rest of the track just seems to fall into place.

Can you explain any unusual recording techniques you have used to capture a particular sound?

Gerry: Carpeted rooms can be quite dead for stringed

instruments like guitar and fiddle, so sometimes I'll put down a piece of plywood on the floor, then get Lisa or myself to stand on that when playing, to capture some early reflections which can liven up a string sound.

Also, for the track 'Dew Is On The Grass', we put a mic on Lisa's foot tap which really drives the performance. When I first started recording I used to take off my shoes or put a cushion on the floor so that the foot taps wouldn't spill onto the mic sound, but now I'll try and make it a feature if it's integral to the performance. So I might put a floorboard down and mic the sound of that.

Do you use any unconventional instruments, or take samples from 'the world around you' to use in your music?
Lisa: We used quite a few unconventional instruments for the album (though they're probably not so unusual within the traditional music scene), because I really wanted to explore different musical textures. So we have a hammered dulcimer, an autoharp, plucked fiddles/viola, recorder, uilleann pipes. We used a sample of stones and some crackling fire for a track called 'Bitter Withy', on which we also used some whispers. I would definitely like to explore samples more but I wanted this album to be quite instrument based.
Gerry: Lisa really wanted to get away from the usual suspects in terms of instrumentation, so there is very little guitar at all, which is quite unusual for a folk album. Autoharp and dulcimer panned left and right

tended to take over the guitar role and we also used a set of live timps, again to get away from the usual things you'd expect.

Do you enjoy recording at home? If so, what's so special about it?
Lisa: I do enjoy recording at home for a few reasons. Firstly, because you are in the comfort of your own home, which allows you a lot of flexibility and freedom, and, secondly, you are not having to pay for expensive studio time.

Do you think musicians/producers can generate album-quality material at home, or is it better to use a studio?
Lisa: I definitely think they can but I think it depends what you're doing and how tolerant your neighbours are.

Can you give one or two recommendations to other people who are getting into recording music at home?
Gerry: Get a good mic! Don't skimp on this! Learn your software inside out. Learn how to mic things properly.
Lisa: Learn when to stop and move on.

Pro Tools

Pro Tools is one of the most established and well-known pieces of audio recording software. Built by a software company called Digidesign, it is cited over and over again as the home musician's companion of choice and can cost as little as £250, which isn't that far out of reach for most people.

It does come with some problems, as a few of the people who contributed to this book will tell you: some prefer to record their instruments into Pro Tools, but later edit in Logic because it's easier. Some complain that when they are recording vocals using the Pro Tools M-Powered system there is latency (delay), which prevents you from making a clean recording. However, there's no disputing that it's one of the most popular systems and it's certainly worth a bash or two.

The Pro Tools Systems

There are three Pro Tools systems you can use: Pro Tools HD, LE and M-Powered.

Pro Tools HD is for the big guys: the people who probably make a living out of making music and are paid by the music industry to create tracks and mix and master them direct out of one flashy studio. If you're serious about a career in the recording music industry, then it might be a good idea to start thinking about professional courses, where Pro Tools HD will be among the things you learn about.

The two more accessible versions of Pro Tools available are Pro Tools LE and Pro Tools M-Powered. Pro Tools LE sits in your home computer, while Pro Tools M-Powered is best described as a portable version of the system, all held in one box. Pro Tools LE was recently upgraded and is now available with the Digi 003 Family, what they call the 'Factory' and the 'Rack'. It's basically a bundle of software and hardware that allows you to do all of the following: compose, perform, record, sequence, edit, mix, master and promote your audio creations.

The 003 Factory provides hands-on control of Pro Tools through its integrated control software and offers a wide range of audio and MIDI functions, high-definition audio resolution, virtually the creativity and speed of industry-standard Pro Tools HD software, high-speed FireWire connectivity, over eighty professional instrument and effects plug-ins, sound libraries and services such as online support and help.

The 003 Rack provides all of the above, including audio capabilities and connectivity, but packages everything together in a streamlined '2U Rack', which is basically a very sleek-looking external box. It also includes Pro Tools LE software and comes bundled with over sixty professional instruments and effects plug-ins, compatible applications, sound libraries and online help services. The Digi 003 Family performs all processing on the host's computer, so you will have to ensure that your computer has enough memory to cope with everything – this is something you should check before you buy.

More than likely you will only be creating a certain number of tracks for each song, but Pro Tools LE will handle up to 32 tracks (or 48 with the Music Production Toolkit or DV Toolkit options, which you have to get separately) as against up to 192 in Pro Tools HD – which is obviously very ambitious.

In April 2005, Digidesign released Pro Tools M-Powered, which brought almost all Pro Tools LE functionality to a subset of M-Audio USB, FireWire and PCI interfaces. Sounds complicated? It's not. Digidesign basically made Pro Tools LE compatible with a small, external box into which you can plug your microphone or instruments. It also stores all of your tracks and recording history and many of the effects that you might want to apply to your songs. M-Powered USB, FireWire and PCI interfaces are the connections you will use to merge your instruments, M Box and computer. It is more straightforward than it seems.

If all of this seems a little baffling, if not an expense you'd rather not indulge in, then check out Pro Tools Free, a free online download. It might be wise to get your head around this before making a specific purchase. Pro Tools Free was released as a version of Pro Tools 5x. It is limited to eight audio tracks and 48 MIDI tracks. It will run only on Windows 98/ME and Mac OS 9.

An official Pro Tools training curriculum and certification program was introduced by Digidesign in 2002. It includes a full range of Pro Tools-related courses in music and post production. The curriculum is delivered by a number of schools and universities around the world.

Hardware
Here's an overview of current Pro Tools hardware available to those who want to use one of the HD, LE and M-Powered systems. It might be sensible to research these in more detail before you decide which system is right for you. (Note: I/O stands for input/ output.)

Pro Tools HD
HD 1/2/3 Core Systems
192 I/O (8ch 192kHz interface)
192 Digital I/O (8ch 192kHz interface)
96 I/O (8ch 96kHz interface)
96i I/O (16ch 96kHz interface)
Pre I/O (8-channel microphone pre-amp)
SYNC I/O (Time Code Synchronizer)

MIDI I/O (MIDI interface)
Expansion|HD Chassis

Pro Tools LE
Digi 003
Digi 003 Rack
Digi 002
Digi 002 Rack
Mbox 2
Mbox 2 Pro
Mbox 2 Mini
Mbox

Pro Tools M-Powered, M-Audio interfaces
Audiophile Series
Delta Series
Fast Track USB
FireWire 1814
FireWire 410
FireWire Solo
Black Box
Ozone
MobilePre USB
Ozonic
ProjectMix I/O

Tips for using Pro Tools
These are some small tips I have picked up along the way about
the differences between the different Pro Tools ranges and how

they work with each other. Bear in mind that there are forums dedicated to this on the web, plus various blogs. Some people obviously spend a lot of time using the system and it's wise to go online and check what they say.

- The M-Powered version does not support the DV Toolkit – the software which creates more audio and MIDI tracks for you to play with. Although the M-Powered users can get the Music Production Toolkit option for the increased track count (among other things), the DV Toolkit option is not supported. So, if you are looking to work on post-production projects (that is, mixing, editing and adding effects to your songs), you really should stick with Pro Tools LE for the DV Toolkit and other related perks.

- Pro Tools M-Powered does not include the Pro Tools Ignition Pack – the bundle of free software which includes an array of composition and production tools to help you expand the power and versatility of the system. Pro Tools M-Powered does, however, contain a version of Ableton Live. Ableton Live is a loop-based software music sequencer for Macintosh and Windows, built, unsurprisingly, by Ableton. The latest version of Live, Version 6, was released in September 2006. Live is designed to be as much an instrument for live performances – and will often be seen used by DJs and dance music lovers – as a tool for composing and arranging.

An Alternative to the Digidesign MBox 2

There is another alternative to LE and M-Powered, although it is a little more limited the M-Audio FireWire 410. It is basically a portable box, like the M-Box, with some simple recording options, allowing you four inputs and mixing capability for your songs. On the PC, the 410 is supported by Windows 2000 with Service Pack 3 or later, and XP with SP1 or later, but not under Windows 98 or ME. On a Mac, it's supported by OS 9.2 or later and costs £350.

All About Pro Tools M-Powered

After much research, including the fact that the noisy singer in the room next door to me swears by it, it turns out that Pro Tools M-Powered is probably one of your best options for getting off the ground with home recording, so here's a small start-up guide on how to use it. For more up-to-date and in-depth information, refer to online sound recording forums and websites and the Pro Tools reference guide and www.digidesign.com.

Before proceeding, make sure you have:

- connected the Digidesign-qualified M-Audio interface to your computer, as described in M-Audio documentation.
- installed Pro Tools M-Powered software and the pre-authorised iLok, as described in the appropriate Windows or Macintosh installation chapter of the Pro Tools M-Powered Getting Started Guide.

Getting sound in and out of your M-Audio interface

To hear audio recorded into a Pro Tools session, you will need to connect headphones or an external sound system (such as powered monitors or a home stereo) to your M-Audio interface. Sound from your M-Audio interface cannot be played through your computer's speakers or your computer's sound output.

Connecting headphones

Depending on which M-Audio interface you have, there will be one or more headphone jacks on the front or back of your interface. These can be either a ¼-inch jack or a ⅛-inch mini plug jack. Connect headphones with a ¼-inch stereo connector (or an adapter) to interfaces that have a ¼-inch headphone jack – as you would an ⅛-inch mini in the ⅛-inch jack.

Connecting a sound system

Depending on which M-Box interface you have, the outputs will be ¼-inch or RCA plugs which can be connected to any amplification system: powered speakers, a home stereo system or an audio mixer. When connecting to a stereo system, connect the left channel (often the white plug) to the first output, and right channel (often the red plug) to the second output. The first and second outputs play the audio that is routed to analogue outputs 1 and 2 within Pro Tools.

Connecting audio inputs

For stereo inputs, use the first input for the left input, and the second input for the right input. For additional stereo inputs, use subsequent input pairs, if available. Home stereo systems often use RCA connectors. You can use an adapter or a special cable to convert from the TRS or TS connectors (used on some M-Audio interfaces) to the RCA connectors on your home stereo.

Connecting a microphone

There can be several ways to use an M-Box with a microphone, depending on the type of microphone and cables you use, and the type of M-Audio interface. Some microphone cables use an

XLR connector to attach a microphone to an input; other micro-phones use a ¼-inch connector. If you have a choice, use an XLR connector to connect the microphone to your M-Audio interface to yield better results.

To use a microphone that has an XLR connector:

● if your M-Box has a Mic/Line switch, press it to its out position.

To use a microphone that has a ¼-inch connector:

● plug the ¼-inch connector from your microphone into one of the Mic (or Mic/Inst) ¼-inch inputs on your M-Box.

If your M-Box has a Mic/Line selector, press it to its 'out' position.

If your M-Box has a Signal Gain control, carefully turn the input control to the right to increase the input level of your microphone signal.

Connecting instruments to an M-Box

Instruments such as electric guitar or electric bass usually have a lower level of output than instruments and electronic audio sources such as mixers, samplers, keyboards, turntables and synthesisers.

To use a guitar with your M-Box

Plug your guitar cable into one of the inputs on your M-Box.

If your M-Box has a Mic/Line selector, press it to its 'out' position.

If your M-Box has a Signal Gain control, carefully turn the control for the input to the right to increase the input level of your microphone signal.

To use a keyboard or mixer with your M-Box

Plug your keyboard, mixer or other audio source into one of the inputs on your M-Box. On M-Box interfaces that have separate inputs for lower level sources (such as guitars) and line level sources (such as keyboards), use the inputs that support your source. If your source is stereo (such as a stereo keyboard or the stereo output from a mixer), connect the left channel (often the white plug) to the first input, and the right channel (often the red plug) to the second input.

Recording a Pro Tools M-Powered session

Before you record with Pro Tools M-Powered, you first create a Pro Tools session, then prepare an audio track for recording.

To create a Pro Tools session:

1. Verify the connections between your M-Audio interface and your instrument or microphone.
2. Launch Pro Tools.
3. Choose File > New Session.
4. Choose where you want to save your session.
5. Type a name for your session.
6. Click Save.

To prepare an audio track for recording:

1. Choose Track > New.
2. Specify 1 Mono Audio Track in Samples, if your source is mono, or 1 Stereo Audio Track in Samples, if your source is stereo.
3. Click Create.

4. Make sure the Mix window is open by choosing Window > Mix.
5. In the Mix window, click the Audio Input Path selector on the new track. (A mono instrument uses one input on an M-Audio interface, and a stereo instrument uses two. Creating a stereo track in Pro Tools will not make a mono instrument into a stereo instrument. If a mono instrument is recorded on a stereo track, one of the sides of the stereo track will show no signal.)
6. From the pop-up menu, select the interface input you want to record. For example, select Mic/Line 1 if your audio source is plugged into the first input of your M-Audio interface.
7. Play the instrument or sound source at the volume you will record.
8. Use the Signal Gain controls on your M-Audio interface (if any) to maximise the signal going into Pro Tools while avoiding clipping. (Clipping occurs when you feed a signal to an audio device that is louder than the circuitry can accept. To avoid clipping, adjust the Signal Gain control, if any. If the M-Audio interface has front panel Clip LEDS, adjust the gain to a level where the Peak LEDs do not light.)

To record an audio track:
1. Click the Track Record Enable button.
2. Choose Window > Transport to display the Transport window. Click Return to Zero to go to the beginning of the session.
3. Click Record Enable in the Transport window to arm Pro Tools for recording. The Record button flashes red to indicate that Pro Tools is ready to record.

4. When you are ready to start recording, click Play or press the spacebar.
5. Record your performance.
6. Click Stop in the Transport window or press the spacebar when you are finished recording.

To play back a recorded track:
1. If the track's Record Enable button is lit, click on it to take it out of Record mode.
2. Click Play in the Transport window or press the spacebar to start playback.
3. Click Stop in the Transport window or press the spacebar to stop playback.

Importing audio from a CD for mixing or sampling
To import audio from a CD:
1. Launch Pro Tools.
2. Choose File > New Session.
3. Choose where you want to save your session.
4. Type a name for your session and click Save.
5. Put the source CD into your computer's CD drive.
6. Open the Workspace browser by choosing Window > Workspace. The Workspace browser is a window where you can find, audition and manage your audio files.
7. In the Workspace browser, click the Audio CD icon to show the files on the CD.
8. Click the speaker icon in the Waveform column to audition the audio file. Press the spacebar to stop playback.
9. Drag the audio file from the Workspace browser to the Track

List in the Edit window to import the file to a new audio track.

To play back the new track:
1. In the Transport window, click Return to Zero to go to the beginning of the track.
2. Click Play in the Transport window to begin playback.
3. Click Stop in the Transport window or press the spacebar to stop playback.

Creating an audio CD from a Pro Tools session

Pro Tools does not create audio CDs directly, but you can create stereo audio files from your Pro Tools sessions, which can separately be burnt to CD. To do this, follow the instructions below.

Bouncing (sending) audio to memory:
Use the Pro Tools Bounce to Disk feature to combine all your audible tracks into a single 'master' audio file. After the new audio file has been bounced to disk, you can burn it to a CD. If you are bouncing down audio from 24-bit resolution to 16-bit (CD resolution), you should use a dither plug-in on the main output. (For details, see the Pro Tools M-Powered Getting Started Guide.)

To bounce audio to disk:
1. After you have finished recording and mixing a session in Pro Tools, select the length of the session in the timeline ruler (or on a track), plus an additional amount of time to avoid cutting off any reverb tails (the echoing sound) that might continue past the end of the song.
2. Choose File > Bounce to > Disk.

3. In the Bounce Options dialogue box, choose Outputs 1–2 as the Bounce Source.
4. Choose BWF (.WAV) for the File Type.
5. Choose Stereo Interleaved for the Format.
6. Choose 16 for the Resolution and 44100 for the Sample Rate.
7. If you are changing the sample rate of the bounced file, choose a Conversion Quality setting. (For details, see the Pro Tools M-Powered Getting Started Guide.)
8. Choose Convert after Bounce, and click Bounce.
9. In the Bounce dialogue box, give the bounce tracks a name and choose where they should be saved.
10. Click Save. Pro Tools begins bouncing to disk. Pro Tools bounces are done in real time, so you hear audio playback of your mix during the bounce process (though you cannot adjust it).

Burning a CD
After the bounce is completed, you will have an audio file that is ready for burning to a CD. Quit Pro Tools and launch any common CD burning application to burn your bounced mix. Make sure you configure your CD burning application to create an audio CD rather than a data CD.

Controlling delay (latency) during monitoring
Pro Tools M-Powered uses your computer for all audio processing, playback and recording. This causes a small amount of audio delay, or latency, in the system. Latency is most obvious when

you are listening while recording. You may hear this as a slight delay between when you produce the sound and when you hear the sound through the speakers or headphones.

Pro Tools hardware buffer

One factor contributing to latency is related to the hardware buffer size in Pro Tools – the larger the buffer size, the larger the latency. You can reduce the amount of monitoring latency for Pro Tools systems by reducing the hardware buffer size. However, even at the smallest buffer size, there is still some latency. In addition, reducing the buffer size limits the number of simultaneous audio tracks you can record without encountering performance errors, and reduces the number of plug-ins you can use.

While there may be times when you want a larger buffer size, for the sake of higher track counts with more plug-ins, you will generally want a smaller buffer size when recording audio that is monitored through your Pro Tools system.

To set the hardware buffer size:
1. Choose Setup > Playback Engine.
2. Choose the buffer size (in number of samples) from the H/W Buffer Size pop-up menu.
3. Click OK.

M-Audio Control Panel mixer

If your M-Audio device has a Control Panel mixer with a direct monitoring feature, it is possible to use this feature as a low-latency monitoring path while recording in Pro Tools.

To use the M-Audio mixer direct monitoring feature while recording:

1. In Pro Tools, record-enable the tracks you want to record and mute their output.
2. Open the M-Audio Control Panel for your MAudio interface. (If you are monitoring the recording source with an external mixer, before it is routed to Pro Tools, you will not hear any latency. Computers with slower CPUs may not be able to use the 128-sample buffer size without encountering performance errors.)

Davey MacManus – lead singer, The Crimea

The Crimea began life as The Crocketts, signing to a UK major label, V2, in 1998 and releasing two albums, but in late 2001 the band was dropped from the label's roster as part of a 'rationalisation' plan. Unwilling to quit following this setback, Davey MacManus and Owen Hopkin formed The Crimea. Comparing The Crimea to their former band, an early press release said, 'If The Crocketts were four cavemen banging stones together, [then] this is the sound of four Tchaikovskys banging Kylie Minogue'.

The Crimea was signed to Warner Bros Records following a showcase at the 2004 SXSW Festival in Texas. Their debut album, *Tragedy Rocks*, was released in 2005, with the first single from the album, 'Lottery Winners

>>

On Acid', released on 9 January 2006; it entered the UK singles chart at no. 31 and became the first of three singles to appear as Single of the Week on what was then the show hosted by both Colin Murray and Edith Bowman on BBC Radio 1. In support of their second single, 'White Russian Galaxy', the band performed on *Top of the Pops*.

Owing to poor album sales, Warner Bros dropped The Crimea in late 2006. Displaying remarkable tenacity, the band continued to write new material and in April 2007 released *Secrets of the Witching Hour* as a free download from the band's website; a CD was also available, with artwork by Joe Udwin, the band's bassist, in collaboration with the London-based visual artist Tersha Willis. The band received a lot of support from Radio 1 DJ Colin Murray, who gave The Crimea airtime on his nightly show by playing one track from the album each week and advocating downloading the album. The band hoped to tour substantially off the back of the new record.

The Crimea have toured with artists including Regina Spektor, Billy Corgan and Ash. During December 2006 the band played three dates in support of Snow Patrol on their UK arena tour ending at Wembley Arena, London.

Do you record music at home/ have you ever recorded music at home?

We recorded our last two albums mostly at home, but more specifically on the latest album – all the vocals and mixing were done at home, as well as most of the instrumentation.

>>

Can you explain what kind of music you make?

We make multi-layered countrified pop/rock music with a left-field approach. Sonically it sounds like Beck or Coldplay with a 60s tinge. The sound varies considerably but no style is feared when recording in the home environment, as you have limitless time to mess about.

What equipment/software do you use to record music at home?

We use a Pro Tools set-up to mix on, and a Roland 1680 for recording and getting up sounds, alongside Dynaudio speakers and whatever instrumentation, keyboards etc. we can get our hands on. In terms of other outboard equipment, we use very little, although we did borrow several different pre-amps for the making of our last album. After everything on the album was recorded we ran it all through a Neve channel-strip to give it a more earthy sound.

How do you go about recording vocals at home?

I use the vocal compressors and EQs on my Roland 1680 to get up a sound, and record straight into that or Pro Tools. I have a Neumann microphone and built a vocal booth with some old duvets – I'll move around in it to get a good sound. My neighbours sometimes complain so I try and keep the front garden looking nice.

How do you go about recording instruments/percussion at home?

We put the amplifiers in the cupboard under the stairs to

get some separation, then we record through a pre-amp and sometimes a compressor. As you have millions of channels on Pro Tools, we usually record about three tracks of everything, e.g. direct-in and two different mics on the amp, then choose later, or make one supertrack of all three sounds. We record instruments right in front of the desk, listening to the finished sound, then we chop the hell out of everything in Pro Tools.

Do you use samples, or pre-recorded beats?
We do steal bits or ideas, or just record whatever it is into Pro Tools and then move it around rather than sampling. We have a drummer, and if we need to loop something we just do it with Pro Tools – it's pretty old fashioned how we do it, but mostly on this album it involved getting the sound right before we recorded it.

Do you enjoy recording at home?
You have as much time as the pace of your life decrees. There's nobody to tell you what to do, or to use their poxy method, and you can make as much tea as you want and smoke if required. You can work as late as you want without fear of running up a massive bill.

Do you think musicians/producers can generate album-quality material at home, or is it better to use a studio?
There is no longer a standard quality. People spend half their lives trying to make stuff sound scuzzy and old and

the easiest way to do this is at home with crappy old gear and the sound of the door creaking endemic on every track.

Do you have a record/publishing deal? If so, who with?
We have a publishing deal with Warner/Chappell. Our latest album has been released as a free download from thecrimea.net. We are hoping for as many people to hear it as possible, the idea being that we make money from selling the hard copy, touring and merchandise.

Can you give one or two recommendations to other people who are getting into recording music at home?
Take your time, try every single possibility till you find the right one, be extremely patient, police yourself, stop and listen to what you are doing, tell yourself it's terrible, change it a million times, finally finish with something you hate. Worry about it for a day, then change it all again, cut it up and stick it back together all wrong, but somehow it works, and you have a gift, a song – it's like home birthing.

Can you give me your favourite recording anecdote?
We decamped to the wilds of Norwich with our own studio and spent three weeks recording all day and all night. We pulled the caravan into the field away from the house, and I used it as my singing booth. Joe and Andy N worked on bass and guitars, whilst Andy Stafford worked mathematic equations, arranging intricate melodies upstairs in Studio

Three. We kept those three home studios going non-stop, one of which was the trusty old 16-track we made *Tragedy Rocks* on, constantly refining parts, sounds, words. It was our special time away from the sh*tstorm of London.

Once I had to leave and rushed across to Bristol for a funeral. I felt like a caveman in the real world, awake in the daytime, my Scott-of-the-Antarctic beard full of breakfast like the Twits. I had to then sign on in Camden, and make it back to the safety of the countryside which involved cycling nine miles home in the pitch black, barely able to see the road and several times colliding with the ditch. I stopped to light a cigarette out on the Broads. Not a sound around. Through the fields I saw the lights of the house where our album *Secrets* was fleshed out. Everything was done at breakneck speed; it was a race against time, as we wanted to release it on Christmas Day. We were beginning to get cabin fever, lose control of our minds.

We finished the brunt of the music, returned to a studio in Brick Lane to record strings and all the weird instruments. One night we invited all our friends down to form a choir of sorts. Only about fifteen people turned up, which reminded us how out of touch we had become. We didn't have any friends left, but we knew what we wanted. We didn't have the posh equipment and, only armed with the secret formulae, we began to mix and construct the viaducts of our dreams. Every day from 12 a.m. till the smallest hours we mixed at my house in a blazing stupor. Taking turns at the controls of the whale, deep behind its Perspex eyes we guided her back to the hunting grounds.

>>

> Trying twenty different sounds for every piece of music till we found the one that blended, obsessing on the tiniest things till our heads were ringing, and we couldn't tell our ass from our ears. One month later the thing was done. The whole process had been a six-month odyssey/travesty, but it sounded how we wanted and that was all that mattered.

Logic

Logic Express 7 is Apple's flagship home recording application, used by many types of people, from hobbyists all the way through to professional recording artists. It's going to set you back in the region of £500, but like all Apple creations it seems to be treasured by those who use it.

In order to use Logic Express 7, you will need the following:

- an Apple Mac computer with an Intel or PowerPC G4 or G5 processor
- 512MB of RAM
- Mac OS X v10.4.3 or later
- QuickTime 7.0.3 or later
- 6GB of available hard drive space
- DVD drive for software installation
- low-latency multi-input/output audio hardware and MIDI interface recommended

Using Logic with a PC: some people out there think that it's possible. It's a rather daunting scenario, though, with endless blogs and forums dedicated to how you might achieve this.

Some folks have managed to run a version of Apple's operating software OS X on their PCs, which would allow you to operate Logic. However, if you are a beginner, we would suggest that you keep the recording process as easy as possible. This is no easy task – so, if we were you, we would avoid it altogether.

Furthermore, before we start to tell you some of the benefits of using Logic, it's important to point out that this can be an overwhelming subject – there is an awful lot to learn if you are going to get the most out of your system. The best thing to do is to look online at home recording websites; one we would recommend is Sound on Sound, where lots of experts will direct you to special articles and books about the subject.

So, what can Logic do?

Logic contains more than fifty software instruments and plug-ins, and offers precise control over recording, editing and mixing. It's also perfect for GarageBand users seeking to step up to a more advanced application, with a studio-style mixer and the ability to edit and print performances using standard music notation.

The layout of the application is extremely flexible, so it shouldn't be too difficult for you to pick it up and navigate a session within a couple of tries. It is easy to get off the ground with Logic, but using it in a more professional manner will require some solid reading and even some online lessons. Some colleges even teach students how to use Logic – it can be an in-depth subject.

Logic Express enables you to record up to twelve instruments, voices and more, all at the same time. Then you can adjust and edit each of these tracks to present the best musical performance possible. Tracks can be saved at high-resolution 24-bit/96kHz as Apple proprietary files or MP3.

What follows is a rundown of some of Logic's best features.

Sample editor

A powerful Sample editor is incorporated in Logic Express 7, allowing precise editing of your audio data. Beyond simple operations such as cut, copy and paste, an extensive suite of DSP (digital signal processing) tools is also available. These tools include time stretching, pitch shifting, and formant correction. In the Sample editor, you can correct improper timing (or adjust the timing) of your audio recordings, translate pitched monophonic audio recordings into notation, or extract the rhythm of an audio drum loop for use as a quantisation template on MIDI performances.

Arrange

The Arrange window – or simply the Arrange – forms the heart of Logic Express 7. This is where you typically record and arrange your music. All audio and MIDI data, including Apple Loops, used in your song are represented as graphical objects. These objects can be moved and edited in multiple ways to form an elaborate arrangement. Audio recordings and MIDI keyboard performances are captured and displayed in a linear fashion, vertically divided into tracks.

Mixer

The Track Mixer in Logic Express 7 controls a maximum of 255 audio tracks, 64 audio instrument tracks and a nearly unlimited number of MIDI tracks. Each audio and software instrument track can display and use up to fifteen insert plug-ins. It also features a core collection of 26 software instruments.

Loops

Remixers and electronic music composers can't live without loops. Logic Express 7 has the same Apple Loops browser as GarageBand, hosting a multitude of Apple Loops. The library is pretty extensive (that's an understatement!) and loops can be pre-selected by choosing mood or genre. What's more, you can use the Apple Loops Utility to construct your own Apple Loops from conventional audio files, such as recordings you have made elsewhere or created in Logic itself.

Apple Loops are visible in the Audio window, can be dragged onto an audio track and are edited in the same fashion as other audio files. It's also possible to edit the loops so that they match the master key of the song, through real-time pitch shifting, which is easy to come by on the menu.

Software instruments

For those more advanced, Logic contains 25 synthesisers and the samplers provided in Logic Express are a priceless resource. The instruments are easily inserted into an audio instrument channel strip in the Logic Express 7 mixer. The integrated track-based automation system allows you to graphically display and edit the duration of each sample. If you have an external mixer, you can adjust and record the parameters of the samples using real knobs and faders, which sync up with Logic.

Effects plug-ins

Forty effects plug-ins are included in Logic, which Apple say can help you to 'conceptualise and realise your sound design visions with a minimum of fuss'.

Here's a list of some of the features available to Logic users.

Notation

The Score editor perfectly transforms MIDI performances into notation. Professional notation printout functions allow you to quickly deliver anything from a lead sheet to a complete orchestral score. Automatic transposition of different instruments is supported, as well as guitar tablature, drum notation and rapid entry of song lyrics or performance notes.

Music for video

Logic Express 7 offers a variety of features that allow you to add music to video. Synchronisation to QuickTime movie files is provided. Watch a QuickTime movie in a floating window on your desktop and create music with frame-accurate synchronisation. You can also choose to display the video track as a series of thumbnails in the Global Tracks of the Arrange window.

Guitar Amp

The Guitar Amp plug-in enables guitarists to play their instrument through faithful re-creations of guitar amplifiers and speakers, directly in Logic Express 7. The guitar must be connected to your Mac either with an appropriate cable, plugged directly into the audio input on the Mac, or via an additional USB, FireWire cable or PCI-based audio hardware interface.

Logic also offers a wide range of legendary guitar amplifier sounds and a number of different speakers that can be freely combined. As with all other Logic Express 7 plug-ins, Guitar Amp can be inserted in any audio or audio instrument channel for sound processing. This makes it a worthwhile distortion effect not only for guitar but also for any other type of sound.

Compressor
The practical AutoGain feature ensures that a normalised input signal results in a normalised output signal, regardless of the threshold and ratio levels, so you don't lose any of the tone or volume.

Preset Multipressor
The Preset Multipressor is a mastering tool that maximises the loudness of your production without audible side effects.

AAC support
Logic Express 7 now supports the Advanced Audio Coding (AAC) format, Apple's version of the MP3, which is considered to be better compression than MP3. AAC is directly supported by iTunes, making it easy to transfer your songs to iTunes and the iPod, should you want to, although this is possible using normal MP3 anyway.

New Arrange window edit modes
The main working window in Logic Express 7 is the Arrange, which provides the best overview of a project. You use the Arrange to move and edit MIDI or audio regions in order to arrange your song. An integrated channel strip allows direct access to mixing

parameters. Logic Express 7 further refines the capabilities of the Arrange window with additional editing modes:

- Shuffle mode keeps regions from overlapping by restraining movement in relation to other regions.
- Crossfade mode automatically applies crossfades to over-lapping regions.

Project file management

This gives you the ability to manage all project-dependent files in Logic Express 7. You can easily consolidate all audio files, MIDI data, song files, plug-in and instrument settings and movie data into a project folder. You can also create a project folder at the start of a project and have all imported media automatically copied or moved into the folder in the background as you work.

Caps Lock Keyboard

The Caps Lock Keyboard feature takes advantage of your QWERTY computer keyboard to let you input note data – including velocity information – without a MIDI keyboard. Simply jot down melodies and chords using your computer keyboard.

External Instruments

Using your traditional instruments, such as guitar and bass, is designed to be as easy as using internal instruments, with the External Instruments Input/Output plug-in. It automatically monitors the correct audio inputs when an external MIDI device is selected.

Logic key commands

Users of Logic on an Apple Mac will insist that the key commands make recording a lot easier. Here's a list for you to refer to should you buy Logic and want to get off the ground as soon as possible.

Using a mouse is often very intuitive, but it is slow, and to really make the most of your recording session, learning Logic's key commands on the QWERTY keyboard is a worthwhile experience.

Option-K will open Logic's key commands window, which shows you which key shortcuts are assigned to your system. Here you can freely assign key combinations to most of Logic's functions, should you want to.

Useful key commands

Command – Key
Record – *
Play – Enter
Pause – .
Stop – 0
Play or Stop – spacebar
Rewind – [
Forward –]
Solo – S
Metronome – C
Zoom Window Horizontal Out – Control-Left Arrow
Zoom Window Horizontal In – Control-Right Arrow
Zoom Window Vertical Out – Control-Up Arrow
Zoom Window Vertical In – Control-Down Arrow

Open Arrange Window – Command-1
Open Track Mixer – Command-2
Open Score Editor – Command-3
Transform – Command-4
Open Hyper Editor – Command-5
Open Matrix Editor – Command-6
Open Transport – Command-7
Open Environment – Command-8
Open Audio Window – Command-9

Jim Moray

Jim Moray is a singer, multi-instrumentalist, arranger and producer who has created startlingly contemporary recordings of England's traditional folk songs which have been described as the most significant development in folk music in the last thirty years. Since graduating from Birmingham Conservatoire in summer 2003, Moray caused a revolution in the folk world with the release of the album *Sweet England*. In February 2004 at the Radio 2 Folk Awards, in an unprecedented move for a previously unknown artist, he was presented with the BBC Radio 2 Album Of The Year award for *Sweet England*, as well as the BBC Radio 2 Horizon Award 2004 for best newcomer.

In November 2004 Jim was once again nominated for a BBC Radio 2 Folk Award 2005 with his track 'Cuckoo's Nest', recorded with The Oysterband for the album *The Big Session Vol. 1*, which was nominated for Best Traditional

>>

track, a category in which Jim had two nominations in 2004.

In 2006 Jim released an eponymous album, which led to coverage in most of the UK's national newspapers, sessions on BBC radio, a sell-out UK tour, no. 30 in HMV's album of the year poll and a listing in Paul Gambaccini's album of the year programme at the end of 2006. He's probably having a little rest now and being interviewed for books like this.

Do you record music at home/have you ever recorded music at home?

I've recorded two full-length albums including three singles at home. I'm currently working on a third.

Can you explain what kind of music you make?

I am a folk musician.

What equipment/software do you use to record music at home?

I use mainly Logic Pro on a Mac. I have lots of microphones, old and new, and a few different pre-amps. I also have lots of instruments (guitars, drums, pianos, old keyboards) and pedals, amps and effects units to play with.

Do you mix and master your own records?

Yes, both, although to term it mastering would be incorrect – mastering is matching all the songs in a particular CD or playlist together sonically. Most importantly, it

>>

involves a fresh pair of ears listening to the tracks and checking them over in a very accurate listening environment. I'm nowhere near experienced or well-equipped enough to do that.

How do you mix your own records?
Simplistically, I twiddle some knobs till it sounds good, then click 'burn this disc'. In a more complex way, I do whatever is appropriate to the recording I'm making and then I capture the sound I want on a CD. Mixing is overrated, especially in-the-box rather than using outboard equipment. By the time I'm finished tracking I have a fairly complete mix that only requires minimal tweaking. The art is in getting to that stage in one smooth movement without having to pull all the faders down and start balancing again. That's the place where you lose perspective on the sound of the whole.

How do you go about recording vocals at home?
Put the right microphone for the singer's voice in front of the singer, in a room that makes them feel comfortable singing in. There aren't any rules, just strategies that have worked in the past.

How do you go about recording instruments/percussion at home?
See above. I try to make the instruments make the right sound in the room and then put a microphone wherever it takes to make the same sound (or better) come out of

>>

the speakers. The goal is to make the process invisible – nobody is going to listen to your song for the clever bass sound. They'll listen because the song gives them a good feeling to listen to. Concentrate on playing in a way that imparts feelings to the listener and then record it in a way that doesn't screw up the hard work you've already put in. Put another way, potential listeners are listening to music, not recording.

Do you use samples, or pre-recorded beats?
I only really use my own samples nowadays. I make my own drum loops and string phrases to use, but I record them myself. I don't use anything off the shelf for anything that will get released.

Can you explain any unusual recording techniques you have used to capture a particular sound?
Every day is another chance to draw up a new blueprint. Nearly everything I do involves the same old microphones and cables and pre-amps, so in that way there's no such thing as unusual since the usual way of working is to experiment. Ninety-nine per cent of the work happens before the sound reaches the microphone though.

Do you use any unconventional instruments, or take samples from 'the world around you' to use in your music?
Some people would call some of my instruments unusual, but they are very common in English folk music. I have

>>

been doing lots of recording of melodeon and hurdy gurdy for my next album, and blending it with programmed drums and electric guitars.

Do you enjoy recording at home? If so, what's so special about it?

I honestly don't think there's anything special about recording at home. The good aspects (being able to work at any time, not be pressured by the clock ticking, being comfortable in your surroundings) are cancelled out by the bad (never having to commit to anything, constant interruptions, being 'too comfortable' to produce anything inspiring).

Do you think musicians/producers can generate album-quality material at home, or is it better to use a studio?

It doesn't matter where you record. It doesn't particularly matter what equipment you use, so long as you know how to get the best out of it. If you feel more comfortable singing or playing at home then that's the best place to be. Sometimes, being in a studio costing money by the hour focuses the mind. In which case, that's probably the best place to go.

Do you have a record/publishing deal? If so, who with?

I'm published by Warner/Chappell. I release records through a company called Weatherbox, but it's not a traditional label/artist relationship.

Fruity Loops (FL Studio)

www.flstudio.com

FL Studio (formerly Fruity Loops) is a digital audio workstation, programmed by Didier Dambrin (also known as Gol), the creator of Image-Line Software.

In researching this I found a lot of people using free downloads of Fruity Loops. The software is especially well known within the music community as a relatively low-cost, user-friendly platform for the creation of hip hop, electronica and dance music, although the complete version contains enough features to handle the production of songs in many different genres.

Music is basically created by recording and mixing audio and/or MIDI data together to create a song, which can then be saved to the program's native .FLP (Fruity Loops Project) format. Songs can be exported to a Microsoft WAV or MP3 file, which are compatible with most media players and computers. FL Studio is a pattern-based music sequencer, with 64 tracks, which allows you to create songs in pieces (patterns) using the Step Sequencer and the Piano Roll view, then merge those pieces using the Playlist window. The Effects Panel provides access to a wide range of software effects which would more often be made available as plug-ins online. Further into this chapter we'll detail some of those effects, so you will have a good idea what's available in general and, hopefully, will be inspired with some ideas for your own songs.

FL Studio is available in three editions, each with a different set of features.

Express Edition is the smallest version, and with the most limited selection of features. It is meant to be used more as a drum machine than as a full-fledged audio production program. This edition of FL Studio is available only for online download.

Fruityloops Edition is the second version and will probably best suit the beginners among you. It is more or less a stripped-down version of the Producer Edition. Available online, it contains a lot of special effects, but not as many, of course, as the latter.

Producer Edition is the highest version, with more features than most people could cope with. This edition of FL Studio is available for online download or box-set purchase.

Fruity Loop's user interface

The FL Studio (regardless which version you are using) user interface comprises five main screens:

1. Step Sequencer – enables quick assembly of drum patterns and short melodic parts.
2. Piano Roll – a two-dimensional grid for composing purposes. The vertical axis represents pitch and the horizontal axis represents time.
3. Playlist – allows the arrangement of sets of patterns and audio files for assembling a complete song.
4. Mixer – used for balancing audio levels, adding effects processors (accessible from plug-ins) and recording audio input.
5. Sample Browser – allows quick access to audio samples, plug-ins, presets and other FL Studio song files (FLPs).

Key features

From version 6.0 onwards, Fruity Loops includes many instrumental effects such as reverb, chorus, flanger (see page 149 for information on flanging) and the like.

Because of widely variable Piano Roll techniques in Fruity Loops, drum sequences can be 'sliced' and rearranged to create breakbeat-style rhythms, as well as other complex rhythms.

The standard version of FL Studio also includes a number of generators (software synthesisers). Some of these must be purchased separately as plug-ins, which are generally inexpensive. The Producer Edition of Fruity Loops includes a mixer and multi-track audio recording capabilities for sound hardware with ASIO drivers (see pages 131–2 for more information). The FL Studio XXL offer includes all optional components with a 40 per cent price reduction. FL Studio uses its own extended internal plug-in, API, to prevent latency, but it can also use VST, Buzz, ReWire and DirectX plug-ins via special adapters, making it compatible with the vast majority of software synthesisers and effects processors.

The demo version of Fruity Loops is fully functional but comes with the restriction of not being able to save projects for later work. It does, however, allow projects to be exported to WAV or MP3 format. Not being able to access full versions of some plug-ins in the program is another drawback of the demo product.

Fruity Loops version 7 onwards also includes sound generators. This is a long list, but to give you an idea of some of the amazing effects Fruity Loops includes, here goes:

- BeepMap – generates unusual sounds from Bitmap image files (.bmp files)
- BooBass – a realistic bass guitar simulation
- FL Slayer – an electric guitar simulator created by Refx
- FL Keys – a multi-sampled synthesiser for various piano sounds
- Fruit Kick – for generating synthesised kick drum/bass sounds
- FPC – software drum machine modelled on the Akai MPC series
- WaveTraveller – useful for record-scratch effects
- FM, RM, VA and plucked-string synthesis, numerous multi-point, tempo-syncable envelopes
- PoiZone – an easy-to-program synthesiser capable of producing a wide variety of trancy sounds
- Slayer II – a guitar simulation that improves upon the included FL Slayer (VSTi plug-in by reFX)
- DrumSynth Live – a complex drum synthesiser
- BeatSlicer easily 'slice' any WAV file (not only loops) into its specific parts and edit those slices
- Deckadance – a powerful DJing tool similar to Traktor DJ
- ASIO drivers (a generic driver, ASIO4ALL, is also included for cards without native ASIO support) to reduce latency
- EQUO – equaliser that can be automated to morph different aspects of sound
- Fruity 7 Band EQ – seven-band equaliser
- Fruity Big Clock – displays song length in various formats
- Fruity Balance – a stereo balance plug-in to create a panning effect; sends different sounds out through left and right speakers

- Fruity Delay – adds delay (echo)
- Fruity Delay Bank – allows complex delay effects by having eight identical banks in parallel, each of which can be fed to another
- Fruity Flanger – applies flanging effect to audio
- Fruity Chorus – creates chorus effect
- Fruity Scratcher – simulates a turntable; load a .wav file and play with it as if it's a record
- Fruity Mute – automates mute
- Fruity Compressor – scales the output volume, making quiet parts louder without causing loud parts to clip
- Fruity Phaser – creates effect similar to flanging, but with a wider 'sweep' effect
- Fruity Reverb – simulates sound reflecting in enclosed space, creating a live feel
- Fruity Wave Shaper – a wave distortion effect which maps input to output values in a graph
- Fruity Squeeze – a distortion effect that adds a gritty feel to sounds such as drumloops

Donal Lunny

Donal Lunny has been at the cutting edge of the evolution of Irish music for almost thirty years and is generally regarded as having been central to its renaissance. Donal has composed music for theatre as well as for TV and film. Recently he has become more involved with contemporary music and is a much sought after producer.

He also designed the first custom-built bouzouki, the prototype of what is now known as the 'Irish bouzouki'.

From the late 60s, when he formed Emmet Spiceland, the first group to break into the pop charts with Irish music, through the 70s and 80s as a member of the influential band Planxty, the high-energy Bothy Band and the trad-rock band Moving Hearts, Donal has revolutionised attitudes to traditional music.

Can you explain what kind of music you make?
I'm a traditional Irish music accompanist/arranger/producer/composer.

Do you mix and master your own records?
In the last two years I've started mixing without the help of experienced engineers, which I've always had in the past. It's a difficult transition.

What equipment/software do you use to record music at home?
Pro Tools Digidesign 002 7.3.

Do you use samples, or pre-recorded beats?
Not so far, though I have assembled percussion loops made from sections of recorded material.

Can you explain any unusual recording techniques you have used to capture a particular sound?
I often use pitched bodhrán for bass with acoustic

>>

instruments, and it works very well, apart from the fact
that the actual duration of the note is quite short. I use
certain reverbs, with modifications, to extend the notes;
also sometimes use Pro Tools to extend the graphic
waveform.

Do you enjoy recording at home? If so, what's so special about it?
Home recording is a lot more relaxed than studio, mainly
because the clock isn't running – though this can be a
powerful catalyst in spurring people to deliver great
performances. Mixing at home is great, because things
are contextualised; it's easy to lose the plot in a studio
with unfamiliarly magnificent playback sound.

Do you think musicians/producers can generate album-quality material at home, or is it better to use a studio?
It depends on circumstances. I think some brilliant
albums have come out of domestic situations, but
frequently everything happened to be just right, and the
musical picture was right there.

Do you have a record/publishing deal? If so, who with?
I have my own publishing company, but purely to look
after my own publishing.

Can you give one or two recommendations to other people who are getting into recording music at home?
Performance is the most important part of the process.

>>

Quality comes next. It's absolutely possible to make a brilliant album at home, though there are many factors involved. Clean recordings are important; background noise or system noise gets in the way. It's like having a clean window to look through, without fuzzy bits that blur the view.

Your favourite recording anecdote?
In '79, the Bothy Band recorded a live album in Paris (*After Hours*): fourteen nights in a place called Palais des Arts, in St Denis, with a 24-track analogue mobile parked outside. We were fairly relaxed about the first night – testing the recording gear, etc. But when we made the eventual choices of the best takes, the first track on the album turned out to be the first piece we played on the first night. In the intro, I made a sound like a rocket taking off into my mic; it had the desired effect and got a laugh from the audience. It's there to be heard at the start of the album. Nothing like a bit of something off-the-cuff ...

Fruity Loops – is it any good?

From the many interviews conducted for this book and from research on key websites and blogs, the general feeling is that Fruity Loops has in the past been accused of having a bad sound engine, but over the past couple of years the company has worked hard to banish that, and most reviews of the product are now extremely flattering.

If you work on a PC, it would seem that FL is the perfect application for Windows. With the recent addition of extra plug-ins, which give you more freedom when it comes to choosing particular sounds or effects (mostly listed above), it has improved itself all the more. Meanwhile, FL supports 32-bit/192kHz audio and ensures that, outside of Pro Tools, you're getting the best possible audio quality available on the market. When you download Fruity Loops, or buy it boxed, you are also guaranteed a lifetime of free updates – a rare but invaluable treat.

Fruity Loops appears to have presets for everything, even things that don't need presets, like compressors and equalisers. The Coolstuff folder even contains a library of songs, uploaded by other users, which can be studied to learn and experiment with all of Fruity Loops' features. You can know absolutely nothing about music production, pick this up and be hammering out songs within the hour. FL will teach it all to you with the double-click of a mouse.

And finally, Fruity Loops offers good value for money. Even the full XXL bundle of FL costs less than a barebones copy of, say, Ableton Live, so when you consider that FL is as fully featured and capable as most hosts on the market today, it's a steal. Add to that the fact that the next version isn't going to cost you anything and it's even more of a steal, as free upgrades are available for a lifetime.

Web resources for Fruity Loops
www.flstudio.com
www.fruityloopers.co.uk
FLstudioForum.com – growing community of Fruity Loops users

FLipside – FL Studio users forum

SectionZ – FL users community founded in 1997, currently home to over 4000 FL Studio projects

WarBeats.com – free video tutorials on FL Studio use, with over a hundred free FL Studio project files for study

FL Studio Tutorials – providing community-driven tutorials and live online help for new artists

createdigitalmusic.com/tag/fruity-loops

Tom Swindells – aka Itchy Kid and half of Mutant Bootie

Tom grew up near Manchester. Ready for new challenges, he moved to London in 2002 where he started work for the house record label Automatic. Meeting various graphic designers and visual artists opened up new opportunities of sound design and music production work for TV and video. Since then Tom has worked on a wide range of projects for various clients including Orange, Living TV, Candy King and Head. Highlights have included the promos for *Missy Elliot's Road to Stardom* on Living TV, channel stings for Trouble TV and recording voice-overs and producing ring tones for the satirical football website englandallstars.com. A promo for Living TV titled 'Planet Pop' won an award at the 2002 Promax awards. In autumn 2005 Tom completed a library music album for West One Music, *Itchy Kid's Dub and Break-beat Sessions*, which has achieved great success, with tracks having

>>

been licensed to the DVD *The Poker Academy* featuring Nick Moran and Mike Reid. Tom's tracks have featured on programmes on various channels in the UK and overseas including BBC1, Channel 4 and various satellite channels. He has albums in the pipeline for both West One and Boosey and remixes for labels such as Ninja Tune, XL, Polydor, Botchit and Scarper, and Fat Fox.

Do you record music at home? If so what?
I produce a wide variety of music at home.

Can you explain what kind of music you make?
My TV and video work is generally written to a brief so the style is very much dependent on the project. I mainly specialise in dance music styles – anything from hip hop, breakbeat and house – but I have also produced a lot of guitar-based material.

Do you mix and master your own records?
I always mix my music myself and generally also do my own mastering, although some of my work has been mastered elsewhere. Mastering objectively can be an awkward process after spending a lot of time on a track, so getting someone else to do it for you can be helpful.

What equipment/software do you use to record music at home?
I use a PC running the following programs:
● sequencing – Nuendo, Sound Forge, FL Studio, Vegas

>>

- plugins – Waves, UAD-1, TC-electronics, PSP
- synthesis (software) – Korg Legacy Collection, Native Instruments FM7
- synthesis (hardware) – Roland JP-8000, Roland SH101
- EMU 1820M audio interface
- 16-channel analogue mixer
- various microphones by Røde, SE Electronics, Shure, Sony
- turntables
- Roland TD-10 V-drums
- Akai S-2000 sampler
- Dynaudio monitoring (speakers)

How do you go about recording vocal at home?
I first set up the recording area, when necessary hanging duvets and blankets to deaden the room sound. Next it is critical to get the vocalist's monitoring set up properly so they're comfortable with the sound they're hearing as they're recording. Each vocalist is different, so working with them closely, making sure they're happy, is the key. Microphone choice is dependent on the vocalist and the track, but I generally close-mic using a large diaphragm condenser, and sometimes will use ambient microphones elsewhere to give more options at the mixing stage.

How do you go about recording instruments/percussion at home?
I use a lot of electronic drums from my Roland V-drums, which are very easy to record as opposed to an acoustic

kit. When recording any acoustic instrument, experimentation with microphone choice, positioning and treating the room is key. When recording I will try to get as many signals recorded from the sound source as possible to give options at the mixing stage. For example, if recording a guitar, make sure to record the DI signal along with the amp sound.

Do you use samples or pre-recorded beats?

Through the years I have collected a large drum library of samples and beats which I use for all projects. I also record myself playing drums, sometimes using the midi info recorded to trigger other drum sounds.

Can you explain any unusual recording techniques you have used to capture a particular sound?

Ambient microphone placement can be very useful. Placing an additional mic in an unusual place can create a very different sound. Using this technique you can record the natural reverb of the space. Experimenting with hallways and stairwells can create great results, even if only used very sparingly for moments in the finished track.

Do you use any unconventional instruments or take samples from the 'world around you' to use in your music?

I use a Sony stereo microphone along with a mini-disc recorder which is very useful for capturing random sound effects. I will also sample and record any instruments at my disposal. One of my current favourites is my thumb piano.

>>

Do you enjoy recording music at home?
Home recording gives you the freedom to spend as much time on a track as you want, as opposed to in a studio where you are constantly aware of the time and cost implications.

Do you think musicians can generate album quality material at home or is it better to use a studio?
With the cost and quality of music equipment constantly improving, results from home recordings can be just as professional as anything recorded in a professional studio. Recording drum kits can be much easier and quicker in a pro studio, but this depends on the nature of the home studio.

Do you have a record/publishing deal?
I have a deal with West One Music with the album I recorded for them. The other work I do is generally on spec, and if they want to use the track I will get a fee. My other TV work is for up-front fees.

Can you give one or two recommendations to other people who are getting into recording music at home?
If using a computer to record, learn your sequencing software as well as you can. Don't waste too much time trying to learn new programs unnecessarily, just concentrate on a few that you're comfortable with. Trust your ears and your instincts rather than trying to follow rules.

>>

>>

A favourite recording anecdote?
Dealing with awkward musicians who keep complaining about the sound, but without knowing what they're on about, can be really frustrating. Try marking a fader on your mixer 'depth' or 'presence' and, as you raise this slowly while they're listening, watch how they're convinced it starts to sound better, when in fact you're doing absolutely nothing!

Sony Sound Forge

First up – if you are in a four-piece band and want to record that killer demo, or some tracks for your MySpace page, then Sony Sound Forge shouldn't really be your first port of call.

Sony Sound Forge is great for creating and manipulating digital audio. It will allow you to record one track at a time, so, for example, you can rig up a microphone to your computer and record via Sound Forge. But if you are looking to plug in a number of instruments and get them all recording at the same time, this isn't for you. But, and this is a really big but, Sound Forge is a fun, easy editor, layered with lots of effects and different ways to manipulate the sounds you have created. Unlike Reason, it does not include 'digital instruments', so if you want to create the sound of a hundred sweeping violins, Sound Forge is not the man for the job.

Also, be a little cautious. Sony are masters at creating software, but to use it you can only work on a PC that operates on Windows 2000 or XP. Make sure you check these things every time. Nothing is more frustrating than buying software, only to find that your computer can't handle it. The most recent edition of Sound Forge on the market is version 9, which you can buy for roughly £70 – not a bad price if this is the only editing software you intend to use.

By the way, if you do fall in love with it (as some have), then you might want to upgrade to Sony's Audio Studio, a solid performer that gets the job done efficiently and includes some nice extras, such as built-in burning and easy uploading to Sony's community site ACIDplanet.com – for roughly £300–400.

So, what can Sound Forge do?

Sound Forge is a simple program designed for simple requirements. It's possible to record your audio live using either a line-in source (your stereo, for example) or a microphone, then chop, equalise, throw in any number of built-in effects and save to a number of formats including MP3, WMA and WAV, or simply burn the audio to a CD. Bear in mind also that this is a video editing software application, which might be handy if you're making a video to complement your song.

Sound Forge sells itself on the depth of its tools, such as delay and chorus effects and even vinyl restoration (for those of you who want to sample tracks from old pieces of vinyl maybe?). It contains what are known as DirectX effects – thirty, in fact, including delay, reverb, chorus, reverse and an easy-to-use equaliser.

It will also handle a number of plug-ins, which can be tweaked by you and then saved as presets for all future recordings. Sound Forge plug-ins include the Flange/Wah-Wah effects and their offshoots Bouncing Flange, Mad Flange and Slow Wah, while EQ presets include Boost Bass, Cut High Frequencies and Cut Midrange. All these plug-ins can be previewed and adjusted in real time (typically there's a delay of a second or two), which allows you to experiment efficiently without applying changes to the track until you are satisfied with the results.

Sound Forge also features the time-stretching and looping tools needed to create samples and loops for the popular ACID Music Studio software. Once the tracks are constructed and optimised, you can drop these files into ACID and create professional-sounding loop- and sample-based tracks that aren't dependent on tempo or pitch.

Setup Sony Sound Forge

According to reports, Windows XP installation is incredibly simple. Along with the main program, you have the option to install the Preset Manager, which offers a simple interface for managing and renaming effects and other plug-in presets. You can also browse 1,001 sound effects, a collection of royalty-free samples and loops that can be saved on your hard drive for easy access.

Sony's free support options come in the form of a FAQ and Forums – there is no one to email and there isn't, sadly, a built-in tutorial. Phone support is available in the US, but it will cost you $14.95 for a single call, $49.95 for 60 days of support or $99.95 for 180 days of support. Not cheap, but then, this is Sony!

Key features
- real-time sample level wave editor
- stereo and multichannel recording
- high-resolution audio support: it outputs 24-bit, 32-bit, 64-bit,192 kHz

- DirectX and VST plug-in support; Version 9 includes a vinyl restoration plug-in and Mastering Effects Bundle
- CD burning
- white, pink, brown and filtered noise generators
- DTMF/MF tone synthesis
- external monitor support for DV and FireWire (IEEE 1394) devices

Sound Forge system requirements

- Microsoft® Windows® 2000 SP4, XP, or Windows Vista™
- 900 MHz processor
- 150MB hard-disk space for program installation
- 256MB RAM
- Windows-compatible sound card
- DVD-ROM drive (for installation)
- supported CD-Recordable drive (for CD burning)

Sound Forge won approval on account of some of the small, seductive bonuses it offers, of which these are particularly alluring:

- access to Sony Music Studios Internet Mastering. Sony gives you the opportunity to have one song mastered free, as long as you pay for another, if not more, to be mastered. It costs $99–$149 per song, depending on your specifications, and Sony promise a 48-hour turnaround. Unless you can get to grips with mastering yourself (it is an art, and many professionals rarely do it themselves), this is a bit of a steal. Professional mastering is not cheap. To learn more, visit www.SonyMusicSIM.com
- Noise reduction. Because Sound Forge is designed to clean up vinyl and digitise music to a high standard, it contains

two plug-ins to deal with common problems such as tape hiss, camera hum, clicks and pops.

- Gracenote® CD album identification. Sound Forge software supports the Gracenote MusicID Media recognition service. When extracting audio from a CD, you can automatically view information including track title and artist, and also save this information to each of your digital files.
- ACID Loop Creation Tools. Acid Loops are looped pieces of music. They were originally created for use with the Sonic Foundry Acid software, but since they are so easy to use, the loops have been made widely available. Sony has taken the ACID software and uses it to help you create your own samples. Using the ACID Loop Creation Toolbar you can display and edit ACID .wav file properties including tempo and root note, finely edit audio clips and shift selections to get the sound you want. When you create a loop, the information you set is embedded in the file, so your loops will change tempo and pitch-shift along with your ACID project.

Soapbox Story

Soapbox Story is also known as Will Hunt, a north London-based singer/songwriter. His first single, 'Lost And Found', was released on 2 July 2007 through Mod Art Sounds. At 18, he went to work with artist/producer Steve Winwood as his apprentice.

Do you record music at home?
After saving what seemed like 200 years of pocket money,

>>

>>

I was able to buy the most basic of Pro Tools home recording set-ups, Pro Tools LE. All I had was a Mac G4, Digi 001, cheap keyboard and a Roland XV5050 sound module. I then went on to record my first solo album, *Entertaining Archie*, learning different techniques of home recording along the way. I was then able to sell these albums at my gigs. The album is now available from any local car boot in Tewkesbury and say hello to Mum while you're there.

Can you explain what kind of music you make?
I think it's difficult to describe your own music but I'm very much influenced by English songwriters like The Jam, Squeeze, ELO, Elvis Costello, The Kinks.

Do you mix and master your own records?
I think mixing and mastering are both very unique talents. Having someone who is able to add to the overall sound and feel of the song is very important, but they must have an idea of what you would like the final result to be, otherwise the reverse can happen. It's always good to take a few of your favourite CDs to the mixing or mastering suite so that your ears can get used to how that room sounds before you start working on your own songs.

What equipment/software do you use to record music at home?
I have a G4, Digi 001, Roland XV5050, Røde K2 microphone, Korg X5D keyboard, guitar POD.

>>

How do you go about recording vocals at home?

It's very difficult to record vocals properly if you don't have a vocal booth to deaden the noise around you, but for recording demos the Røde K2 is an excellent all-round mic for recording both vocals and acoustic instruments. The Røde K2 cost me £375.

How do you go about recording instruments/percussion at home?

Again, the Røde K2 is an excellent mic for this. It's just a matter of experimentation to get the right sound from your instrument.

Can you explain any unusual recording techniques you have used to capture a particular sound?

I used my mouth to mimic a trumpet to create an ambient feel within a track. Putting it low in the mix with lots of reverb opens the tune and the melody line but doesn't distract you away from the song.

Do you use any unconventional instruments, or take samples from 'the world around you' to use in your music?

I have often recorded outdoors or with the window open to capture London noise. If you listen carefully to a couple of my songs, you can hear the boiler kicking in.

Do you enjoy recording at home?

I enjoy recording at home because you have as much time as you need to experiment with your instruments

>>

and recording equipment. You are familiar with your surroundings and it doesn't cost a thing.

Any recommendations?
Spend as much as you can on equipment. It's worth pushing your budget as far as it will stretch. Test the gear before you buy it as you don't want to buy something you will never use. Shop around to get the best deal. Make sure you have a Røde K2 in your mic collection as it's a great mic to start out with.

Propellerhead Reason

Reason is a hugely popular music software application because it is very easy to use. It is one of the few home recording packages that can be plugged in and learned in very little time, mostly on account of its easy-to-use interface. It's particularly popular among the hip hop drum & bass, dub, house, techno, trip hop and trance communities, with luminaries such as The Prodigy's Liam Howlett, Andre 3000, the Black Eyed Peas and even Mike Oldfield claiming that they use Reason to put together songs.

Reason has won praise from users and critics for its original and playful interface. Audio software that mimics hardware was not unknown when Reason debuted, but Propellerhead advanced the concept by allowing users to connect devices via realistically animated cables, making the path of audio and modulation signals through the program easily visible and graspable.

Reason 1.0 was launched in November 2000. It was designed by a Swedish software company called Propellerhead. Small tip: bear in mind that if you do a Google search on this you'll want to type in 'Propellerhead Reason', as opposed to just 'Reason', which doesn't yield any particularly useful results.

Reason does not allow for audio recording. This means you can't plug your guitar or bass into your computer and record through Reason. Only MIDI files can be imported.

So what can Reason do?

The software basically emulates a rack of hardware – synthesisers, samplers, signal processors, sequencers and mixers. Reason can be used either as a complete virtual music studio or as a collection of virtual instruments to be played live or used with other sequencing software. It can be best described as one of the most advanced sequencers out there. It might not be as ideal as Pro Tools for recording actual instruments, but it can achieve a great deal.

There is a free, trial download available online which is a little restricted – Reason Adapted. If you feel that Reason is the software for you, you can buy Version 3 – the most up-to-date version at the time of writing – for roughly £300. Sites you can check include Amazon, Dolphin Music and Propellerhead's website. It is available for both PC and Mac and even works with Windows Vista, which has been criticised for not supporting a lot of software packages.

Nearly everything in Reason can be recorded and automated, from turning dials on synthesisers to twiddling some of the knobs on effects boxes. You can use it as a straightforward MIDI sequencer, playing Reason's instruments from your keyboard and then recording the data. Reason stores all of your tweaks too. You can save a song, come back six months later and all your tweaks will still be there, just as they were when you closed the project the last time. There is only one major thing you can't do with Reason: you can't control external synths with it. That's important if you are considering Reason as a one-and-only sequencer. It can only sequence itself.

Reason version 3.0 includes some of the following modules: two mixers, a subtractive synthesiser, a graintable synthesiser and four different kinds of sample players – one with a step sequencer designed for drums/percussion, two for tonal instruments, and a sliced loop playback device. Effects include distortion, reverb, chorus, a vocoder and mastering effects. The Combinator device, introduced in version 3.0, allows users to combine multiple modules into one.

Reason's features

At this stage, this list of features might not mean anything to you, but it is a useful resource which can be researched at a later date if you are serious about using Reason.

NN-19 Digital Sampler – sample player
NN-XT Advanced Sampler – advanced sample player with velocity-layering and group editing
Dr.REX Loop Player – device for playing loops in REX format
Redrum Drum Computer – pattern-based drum-machine-style sample player
MClass Equalizer (version 3.0)
MClass Stereo Imager (version 3.0)
MClass Compressor (version 3.0)

MClass Maximizer (version 3.0)
RV7000 Advanced Reverb (version 2.5 upwards)
Scream 4 Distortion (version 2.5 upwards)
BV-512 Vocoder (version 2.5 upwards)
RV-7 Digital Reverb
DDL-1 Digital Delay Line
D-11 Foldback Distortion
ECF-42 Envelope Controlled Filter
CF-101 Chorus/Flanger
PH-90 Phaser
COMP-01 Compressor/Limiter
Combinator – utility that combines other devices into a single instrument (version 3.0)
Mixer 14:2 – 14-channel stereo mixer
Line Mixer 6:2 – 6-channel stereo mixer
Spider Audio Merger & Splitter – utility to merge and split audio signals within Reason (version 2.5 upwards)
Matrix Pattern Sequencer

Some useful Reason tips

- The licence allows each user to install Reason on two computers, such as a desktop and a laptop.
- Reason has been highly praised for its stability, with reports of bugs or crashes very rare – an asset that is especially important when using the program in live performance.
- No support for VST and other plug-in effects and instruments.
- No MIDI out, enabling users to control hardware or software instruments from Reason's sequencer.
- Limited 'Undo' action – so try not to mess up too many times, otherwise you could find yourself getting a little angry.

Cubase

Cubase originally started life on the Atari ST in 1989, as the successor sequencer to Steinberg's professional sequencer Pro 24. The company that creates it is now owned by Yamaha. It's one of the veteran pieces of digital recording software and many people have an attachment to it, mainly as a sequencer. It's been claimed that more than a million people worldwide use Steinberg's classic.

Cubase can be ordered online, from a cheap basic version, which will cost you around £90, to a more professional version which costs £250.

As with all sequencers, it creates projects that allow you to edit MIDI files, raw audio tracks, and even other bits of associated information like lyrics, and to present them in a range of formats, which can be burnt onto CD as WAV or MP3 files.

While MIDI is pretty much the standard representation of digital music, there is no broadly accepted standard for the interchange of complete projects containing both MIDI and audio between Cubase and other recording and editing software packages such as Logic, Pro Tools and so on. This means that if you are composing tracks with Cubase, then take that saved project to a friend who is using, say, Pro Tools, the two packages won't be able to communicate information that easily. It is hard to import a whole song, with specific edits, instrument information and automation, in its native format from Cubase to

>>

another application and vice versa. Tracks can be saved sometimes in Cubase's OMFI format and transferred, but people have often remarked that this causes problems.

There have been four main incarnations of Cubase. The original Cubase only featured MIDI and could not handle actual instruments. Cubase VST featured fully integrated audio recording and mixing along with effects, as well as online support and plug-ins. Cubase SX is considered to be a more professional sequencer and audio editor. In September 2006 Steinberg launched Cubase 4, the successor to Cubase SX3. There is another version of SX, SE3, which has been designed for those working from home and on a budget, so that's the one we'll focus on here.

Computer specifications for running Cubase

- MAC: Power Mac G4 867 MHz, 384MB, Mac OS X Version 10.3 or 10.4, CoreAudio compatible audio hardware, DVD drive.
- PC: Pentium/Athlon 800 MHz, 384MB, Windows XP Home or XP Professional, Windows MME compatible audio hardware (ASIO compatible audio hardware recommended), DVD drive.

SE3 offers a budget-priced system for composing, recording, editing and mixing your music. It features a 32-bit audio engine, 24-bit/96 kHz recording and unlimited MIDI tracks. It contains a wealth of audio and MIDI features, powerful editors and a complete set of effects plug-ins to round off its impressive features set.

Cubase features:

- It can handle 48 audio tracks and unlimited MIDI tracks, plus up to 16 VST instrument slots. (VST, or Virtual Studio Technology, refers to an interface standard, created and licensed by Cubase owners Steinberg, for connecting audio synthesiser and effects plug-ins to audio editors and computers.)
- It also contains nifty features such as a video thumbnail track for building your own video soundtracks. (It is used widely in the film editing world for this purpose.)
- It is wise to make sure your set-up has 1GB of RAM to operate Cubase. Two hard drives might even be more helpful – one for Cubase itself and another for saving your tracks when they're complete.

Paul Carter, Flotation Toy Warning

This is the biog we received from the elusive Flotation guys. Safe to say, the band has released records and will be releasing more in 2007.

'First reported sightings of Flotation Toy Warning began towards the later days of the 1760s, as sailors exploring the more westerly edges of the north polar regions made inroads further toward the centre of the subcontinent. Rough sketches appeared in national newspapers, along with a wide range of other fascinating curiosities and strange beasts. But it was not until a full 53 years later

>>

that the first photographic "proof" of their existence was to surface. A blurred print of five (or possibly six) figures crossing what appears to be an area of desert scrub was one of several images offered for sale to the British Museum in September 1820. A Mr Klondike Vasius, who had allegedly taken the photographs during an expedition along the banks of the river Thea, claimed to be in possession of a number of stills that would put the question of Flotation Toy Warning's existence beyond all doubt. These images were later rejected by many as a hoax, although Vasius continued to insist on their authenticity until his untimely death at the hands of Persian bandits in 1852.

'Just two years later saw the emergence of a manuscript amongst a series of letters found in a wine cellar in Bristol as it was being cleared for demolition. The documents, apparently some form of original musical notation for a classical piece to be played by an unheard-of instrument, simply referred to as a "aerophone", have never been successfully translated. Interest in the case waned and Flotation Toy Warning dropped out of the public consciousness for a number of years.

'The beginning of a new century, however, saw the story grab the headlines again, as a Mr Donald Drusky, reputedly an artist and troubadour from Philadelphia, claimed that he was one of the figures in the Vasius stills from 1820. Drusky claimed that Flotation Toy Warning was an experimental project and an ongoing concern, unlikely to see the light of day until the very end of the century. Revered by some academics as the inventor of a new kind of musical style, he was generally dismissed as an attention-seeking eccentric and a crank. Drusky said that the project was a means of documenting human feelings to a degree of realism not previously possible, set to a soundtrack created from previously unknown instruments. The last official documentation of Drusky was medical records detailing his admission to a mental asylum after a breakdown, apparently triggered by experiencing the horrors of trench warfare in the Somme.

'It had been suggested that Drusky was not working alone on the project, and several people came forward in 1938, claiming they had been witness to some form of live music experiment in a Paris factory. Accounts of the events varied wildly, but several versions mentioned a combination of music and film presented by four individuals, one of them apparently using the name Don LeCannes. No further record of either the Paris four or Donald Drusky was uncovered, but Professor Nathanial Worminster, a musicologist based in Sydney, Australia, published a paper in 1995 speculating that the five-piece would emerge again in the next ten years, citing Drusky's 1901 claim that the project would bear fruition in the latter days of the 20th century. Disappointment followed Drusky and his companions failed to materialise before 2000. But then, to the surprise of the academic world, the release of a CD containing at least ten pieces of work was announced in the summer of 2005. The tracks were to be released on Misra Records on 16 August, to be followed

>>

by a series of live "events". Misra had apparently been contacted by an anonymous caller, who forwarded a series of recordings on wax rolls and warned them to expect Flotation Toy Warning, whoever or whatever they were, to emerge from hiding later in the year.

'On the 22 November 2006 items of clothing, music and film were uncovered by Doctor Ernest Shacklewell and are now available for purchase.'

Do you record music at home?

We recorded our first album, *Bluffer's Guide To The Flightdeck*, at home, although home at the time was a large warehouse flat in Dalston – a former clothes factory where I lived for about six or seven years. We wrote and rehearsed all our material there too. The album was eventually released across Europe and the States on several different labels. We also recorded two EPs previous to this.

Can you explain what kind of music you make?

Tough question for any band, really. People sometimes compare us to obscure American bands, but our biggest influence is probably Ennio Morricone. And what we've seen older children doing.

Do you mix and master your own records?

The album was recorded by a guy called Steven Swindon. When recorded, we eventually took it to Bark Studios in Walthamstow, London, and transferred it to 2-inch tape to

>>

warm up the sound. We worked with Brian O'Shaughnessy to mix it. He's done loads of excellent stuff down the years, such as *Screamadelica* by Primal Scream, and he also worked with My Bloody Valentine. Mastering was over in Acton with a guy called Nick – another very talented and experienced person who runs a place called Soundmaster Studios.

What equipment/software do you use to record music at home?

We always use Cubase to write songs on. Now we use it for recording too. But the first album was recorded on Roland digital desks as this was the format Steve Swindon knew best. We started off with a digital 8-track for the EPs which we then connected to a digital 24-track to start the album. Eventually we had to connect both these up to another digital 18-track as one of the songs ('Donald Pleasance') had over 60 tracks on it (string quartets and brass sections take up a lot of space!) and we refused to bounce any tracks down until we got them on to 2-inch tape at Bark.

How do you go about recording vocals at home?

We use an SM58 mic and a home-made pop screen. (This stops the booming and clicking noises you get if you breathe or spit on the mic.). You can make one from an old coat hanger and some tights then attach it to the top of a mic stand. Probably everyone does this – it's not rocket science. And not nearly as kinky as it sounds.

>>

How do you go about recording instruments/percussion at home?

From experience we'd suggest individual mics for string quartet members, as there is nothing more frustrating than a whole recording of a piece being ruined by a few out of tune moments by one player – this way you don't have to scrap the lot and start from scratch. Recording percussion is pretty standard – mic up all the different elements separately if you can. Depends how much freedom you want to leave yourself for the mixing process. If you want a particular lo-fi sound or something then one solitary battered old mic left on the floor in front of the kit can work wonders. But if you later decide you don't like the sound then obviously you're stuck with it.

We tend to mic up guitar amps to record guitars, but put keyboards and samples straight into the desk.

Do you use samples, or pre-recorded beats?

Both. We usually start a song with a borrowed drum loop and home-made samples.

Can you explain any unusual recording techniques you have used to capture a particular sound?

The 'choirs' on one of our songs ('Even Fantastica') are made from sample recordings of three members of the band singing up a stairwell. Since there was no one around to press 'record', it involved triggering it by volume, which meant I had to silently creep down the

>>

>>

creaky stairs before we started recording. I was quiet enough on about the fifth attempt.

Do you use any unconventional instruments, or take samples from 'the world around you' to use in your music? If so, please explain.
Pretty much all our samples are home-made. We use many techniques, often involving singing into a mic put through a myriad of effects pedals to get a keyboard sound. We tend to begin songs by messing around making samples until something interesting happens. You can also process the samples you have made by pitch-shifting them or time-stretching them. Sometimes we've made fifteen-second-plus-long samples which are pretty dull, but you find that a strange noise in the last half second is the interesting bit and just loop that. That's how a song called 'Happiness Is On The Outside' came about.

Your home is also full of useful things to sample. The percussion on one of our songs ('Made From Tiny Boxes') was made by scraping a drumstick around the inside of a metal dustbin and sampling the sound of playing cards being flipped by the spokes of a bicycle wheel.

Do you enjoy recording at home?
There are many upsides and few downsides. Obviously it's free and you can work whatever hours you please. Because it was a warehouse there was no fear of upsetting the neighbours. Recording in a house is much more restrictive. You can make as much tea as you want and

can always leave everything set up to start again the next morning. If, however, the majority of recording is done in what also passes as your bedroom, as it was in my case, it does rather impinge on your privacy and personal space.

Do you think musicians/producers can generate album-quality material at home, or is it better to use a studio?
Yes, absolutely. They can also make a complete pig's ear of it in a swanky studio. It's really down to the skill and imagination of the people involved. With the relatively cheap technology now available there is no reason not to record at home. Having said that, it rather depends on what 'home' is, and the type of music you want to record. If you're a speed metal band and want to record the whole thing live in a modern block of flats, I foresee some problems.

Do you have a record/publishing deal? If so, who with?
We had a record deal for our first album with Pointy Records. The album was then licensed to Misra (US), Talitres (France, Germany, Switzerland, Austria, South Africa, Israel), and Green UFO (Spain). We have a deal for our forthcoming second album with Talitres. We also have a publishing deal for our first album with Talitres.

Can you give one or two recommendations to other people who are getting into recording music at home?
Some people have a natural aptitude for these things and can even record a decent sounding album on a 4-track.

Personally I don't. If you have a friend who is good at these things, get them involved to take responsibility for the technical side. Borrow as much equipment as you possibly can off anyone you've ever met. Get to know someone who plays in a string quartet. Most importantly, always make backups of what you record as you record it.

Can you give me your favourite recording anecdote?
Once, towards the end of a long, long session, we were about to back up what we'd done in the last hour or so. The session was finally finished so we were in high spirits. Whilst dancing along to the playback of what we had just recorded, a member of the band managed to accidentally kick the electric socket out of the wall, completely wiping the last hour's work.

Audacity

Since it was recommended by some of the guys who are profiled in this book, we thought we'd give Audacity a mention. Unlike Pro Tools and Logic, which are full-fledged mini home studios, Audacity is more like Fruity Loops and Reason, which are top-end sequencers.

Audacity is free. Some of the other options we have presented to you are available through free trials, and there are often free limited versions available online, but Audacity is completely free.

You might ask what the catch is. Those among you who are web-savvy will already know about Open Source projects. Open

Source is when one person creates a piece of software and uploads it to the web and people improve on it and re-post it online. This is how the creators of Audacity summarise it: 'Yes, Audacity is completely free, open source software. You are free to use this program for personal or commercial purposes. You are also free to give it away, sell it, or modify it for your own use, under the terms of the GNU General Public License. The authors of Audacity decided to release it under the GPL for many reasons. Some of us do it out of generosity. Some of us do it for moral reasons, because we feel that all software should be free; others believe that there is a place for both free and proprietary software. One reason Audacity is free is so that it will be more popular and useful. Yet another reason is to encourage collaboration. Because of Audacity's free license, dozens of people around the world have contributed code, bug fixes, documentation, and graphics.'

So what can Audacity do?
Here is a brief summary of Audacity's capabilities:

Recording
- Record live audio through a microphone or mixer, or digitise recordings from cassette tapes, vinyl records or mini-discs (handy for sampling!). With some sound cards, it can also capture streaming audio.
- Record from microphone, line input, or other sources.
- Dub over existing tracks to create multi-track recordings.
- Record up to 16 channels at once (requires multi-channel hardware).
- Monitor volume levels before, during and after recording.

Import and Export

- Import sound files, edit them and combine them with other files or new recordings.
- Export your recordings in several common file formats, such as MP3. (Note: Audacity does not currently support WMA, AAC or most other proprietary or restricted file formats.)
- Create WAV or AIFF files suitable for burning to CD.

Editing

- Use unlimited Undo (and Redo) to go back any number of steps. This is one of Audacity's real highlights – unlimited undo is not available on all pieces of kit.
- Fade the volume up or down smoothly with the Envelope tool.

Effects

- Change pitch without altering tempo, or vice versa.
- Remove static, hiss, hum or other constant background noises.
- Adjust volumes with Compressor, Amplify and Normalize effects.
- Other built-in effects include: Echo, Phaser, Wahwah, Reverse.

Sound Quality

- Record and edit 16-bit, 24-bit and 32-bit (floating point) samples.
- Record at up to 96 KHz.
- Mix tracks with different sample rates or formats – Audacity will convert them automatically in real time.

Plug-Ins (for more on this, look at the Plug-in section)
- Audacity includes some sample plug-ins from the creator of plugin.org.uk.
- Load VST plug-ins for Windows and Mac, with the optional VST Enabler.

To run Audacity, you will need the following:
- Windows 98 or better
- sound card with speakers or headphones
- Macromedia Flash installed
- high-speed internet connection

Useful Audacity weblinks
SitePal:
www.sitepal.com
Audacity how-to tutorials:
www.guidesandtutorials.com/audacity-tutorial.html
Audio editing with Audacity:
www.fark.com/farq/audioedit.shtml
Basic guide to using Audacity:
www.mp3soundstream.com/Audacity_Tutorial.html

Music and recording software site SonicSpot.com rates Audacity 97 out of a possible 100 and has Audacity links and information at:
www.sonicspot.com/audacity/audacity.html

Audacity is listed on Update-Scout.com, an interactive web service, which informs its users about software updates and releases. Update-Scout lists open source projects, freeware and shareware.

3

Making the most of your home studio

By this stage, you should have most of the basics under your belt. The actual creation of a song is no doubt the hardest part of recording your own music, and our guide to software and sequencers should have assisted you in making your very first recording. But what happens to your song from here?

Laying down some basic audio and vocal tracks is only the beginning. Once you have completed your recording, it's time to turn that raw file into something people will want to buy or listen to on the radio. There hasn't been one hit song in history which hasn't undergone some form of post-production, and that's what this chapter is all about. All of the hardware and software recommended here will help make your song the killer track you want it to be.

In this section you will learn how to make the most of your studio so that you can add those final touches to your song. One of the most-complained about issues for musicians recording at home is 'latency' or delay – that is, when you replay a song in order to layer tracks, your recording system may cause a delay in the replay of certain elements. Here we show you how to stop that delay from happening.

More importantly, virtually every song that has ever been released in the history of music has been mixed and mastered. You'll discover what those terms mean and why it's vital that you mix and master your own songs.

But it's not all technical processes. There is lots of fun to be had, too. For example, you can use the web to download a vast array of plug-in effects and you can create your own samples to use in your songs. These can be layered onto or built into your finished recording to improve the overall effect. No doubt you've heard a song with a swirling string effect or a brass arrangement, or even stranger noises such as the revving of a car engine or the cry of a baby. Those sounds are all created with the help of plug-ins and samples.

The only thing you really need to know right now is this: be adventurous. You have a raw, saved music file. With that, you can mess around as much as you like. Just be careful not to overwrite it with something you might not like!

ASIO drivers

A common complaint among those recording at home is the problem of delay, professionally known as 'latency'. When you listen back to a song, maybe with the intention of recording more tracks over the top of it, there is often a slight delay in the recording and playback.

A USB ASIO driver is one way to prevent this. It compresses buffer sizes down to 32 samples (0.73 ms) and uses an ultra-high-speed USB audio connection to do so, bypassing the operating system's audio. This gives you not only low latencies but also better quality sound.

SoundManager (Mac) and MultiMedia Extensions (MME/Windows) use non-high-end sample rate conversion in order to sync the different audio signals from applications to the sample rates used on the external sound card. And sometimes there's not even a way to control the rate to be the preferred one (e.g. 48kHz instead of 44.1kHz). You need an ASIO-compatible application like Cubase/Cubasis, Logic Audio/Micrologic, Reason, Live, Digital Performer, Sonar V2.2 or BPM Studio. If the application supports ASIO2 you'll be able to benefit from more features.

Companies including Access, Allen&Heath, Audiotrak, CME, ESI (formerly known as EgoSys), Numark, Sound Devices, Steinberg, Tascam, Terratec and Yamaha decided to license and bundle this driver in with their hardware and software. So fully functional custom ASIO drivers are available for Access Virus TI, Allen&Heath XONE:3D, Audiotrak Maya 44 USB, CME XCORPIO, ESI ESU1808, ESI U24, ESI Gigaport AG / DG, Mindprint DI-MOD USB, Numark DJ IO, Sound Devices USB pre, Steinberg MI2, Steinberg MI4, Tascam US-122L, Tascam US-144, Terratec Area 61, Terratec Phase 26 USB, Yamaha UW10 and Yamaha UW500.

Samplers

A sampler is an electronic device that recreates a sound like an actual instrument. It is virtually like a synthesiser: a box that stores a number of samples which can then be plugged into your digital audio workstation for use on your songs. The sample might be taken from another recorded piece of music, or from something you have recorded yourself from the world around you.

Samples are a collection of sounds that aren't necessarily created from scratch: they can be accessed by ripping (lifting) sections from songs (which can be illegal, depending on copyright issues) or from websites that make samples freely available for you to download and use legitimately.

Normally a sampler is controlled by an attached music keyboard, or from an external MIDI source.

In general, samplers can play back any kind of recorded audio, and most samplers offer editing facilities that allow the user to modify and process the audio and to apply a wide range of effects, making the sampler a powerful and versatile musical tool.

Samplers – a brief history

Before computers existed, engineers would use a keyboard to generate sounds and then record them on to tape for use as samples. One of the earliest machines used to achieve this was the Mellotron: it would only create samples within a three-octave range, but was very prevalent on songs during the 60s and 70s. Modern digital samplers simply recreate what the Mellotron did, although obviously they are far more advanced and you will not be beset by limitations.

Akai pioneered many processing techniques, such as Crossfade Looping to eliminate glitches, and Time Stretch, which allows for shortening or lengthening of samples without affecting pitch and vice versa. The limiting factors in the early days were the cost of physical memory (RAM) and the limitations of external data storage devices. The Akai S900 (1986) was the first truly affordable digital sampler. It was eight-note polyphonic and featured 12-bit sampling with a frequency range up to 40 kHz and up to 750kB of memory that allowed for just under 12 seconds at the best sampling rate. It could store a maximum of 32 samples in memory. The operating system was software-based and allowed for upgrades that had to be booted each time the sampler was switched on.

Your digital audio software will no doubt contain a number of pre-packaged samples for you to drop into your songs at your leisure. Some boast more than 1,000 legitimate samples.

Mattias Olssons – writer/producer/DJ

Mattias Olssons recorded with and produced hundreds of bands such as Änglagård, Wan Light, Pineforest Crunch, Geller and Nanook of the North in Sweden, where he runs his own studio in Stockholm. The Roth Händle studio is the home of one of the world's oddest collection of vintage artefacts and instruments. Optical organs such as the Optigan and Chilton Talentmaker share space together with Benny Andersson's GX-1 and toy pianos under a bicycle repair shop. Mattias Olssons' albums are 'usually based in a very song-driven tradition but are then twisted, flipped backwards and looped into a nice snug three-piece suit,' he says.

Do you record music at home?
I have recorded somewhere between 50 and 100 tracks at home with different artists. Andreas & Jag, Akaba, Pineforest Crunch and Molesome to mention a couple. Some recordings are stranded in the hallway, others turned into albums and singles.

Can you explain what kind of music you make?
It comes from a pop tradition, I guess, but I am a firm believer in contrast and using the wrong sound in the right place.

>>

>>

Do you mix and master your own records?
I mix but I don't master. I try to avoid mixing as I feel that other people do it better. But when I mix I do it very slowly, feeling very angst-ridden.

What equipment/software do you use to record music at home?
I started using a small Akai DPS-12 hard disk recorder which was great because it was incredibly easy to use. It takes five minutes to get it up and running and recording after taking it out from the box. But there are a lot of features one can explore if you are so inclined. After the DPS-12 I bought a second unit and then an Akai DPS-16 and then another 16-channel. The purpose of this was of course to have real physical channels to work with while mixing. This means that I have 52 channels to use while mixing. I want to be able to touch my sounds with faders.

How do you go about recording vocals at home?
I live in a three-room apartment with hard wood floors so we used to find which rooms had the best acoustics for different types of sounds. We usually recorded vocals in the kitchen.

How do you go about recording instruments/percussion at home?
Nothing special ... You avoid doing the loudest stuff at night. Naturally when you record at home there is always the question of volume vs neighbours. Recording music

>>

is usually a pretty loud endeavour so acoustic and miced home recordings usually are quiet and low-key as a result, which has become sort of a trademark.

Do you use samples or pre-recorded beats?
I own Mellotrons, tape-based drum machines, drum machines and Optigans (an organ using optical discs with pre-recorded loops, made by Mattel). These are in a way samples…The difference is that they are on tape and from the 60–70s. In the start we used samples and loops from CDs but I found it to be kind of restricting and I always felt like 'How many other home recordings are done using this exact loop right now?'

I never use samples of real instruments. If I don't have access to a certain instrument or instrumentalist I'll rather use another instrument but with the same function instead.

Can you explain any unusual recording techniques you have used to capture a particular sound?
I use a lot of cheap dictaphone microphones in combination with good stuff to get as much sonic information as possible. One of Sweden's best mixers once told me that mixing is about getting two litres of water into a one-litre bottle. So his main tool when mixing was making sounds smaller where you couldn't hear it.

A lot of the time I think people (including myself) have a tendency to overthink. A couple of weeks back I wanted to make a guitar sound like headphone leakage, so I started rigging different EQs and small speakers until I realised what the most simple solution would be. I took the worst 70s home organ headphones I have and miced them a couple of centimetres apart. And guess what? It sounded exactly like headphone leakage ... quite simply because it was.

I have bought loads and loads of cheap crappy guitar stomp boxes and I still use them on everything. You find your favourites for different things. I have always liked the idea of pushing a button and it changes everything.

Use your rooms as echo chambers (Joe Meek style).

Do you use any unconventional instruments, or take samples from 'the world around you' to use in your music? If so, please explain.
In my studio I have a wide array of different, mostly old and mouldy, keyboards, guitars and effects. I have tape replay keyboards like the Mellotron as well as optical disc organs like the Chilton Talentmaker or the Orchestron. I have been very lucky timingwise, looking for certain instruments and sounds when everyone else thought they were useless and worth next to nothing. I have been given a pipe organ for free and been lucky enough to have room for them.

I have always been interested in using sounds that are viewed as useless because I know that if I take, for instance, a cheap flea-market Casio synth or a home organ and pull it through a distortion pedal and an analog filter, I can be pretty sure that that exact combination will be something that has never been done before. And that makes me excited.

Do you think musicians/producers can generate album-quality material at home, or is it better to use a studio?

I think people should be smart and economic about it. Spend your money where you can hear it. One of the main things that sparked my interest for recording at home was when one of my bands were paying £1000 a day at a studio with a great live room when we were Dling Moogs into the board. For that money we could have easily bought our own Mini Moog. So pick your recording environments for what they do best. If you want to record a great drum sound, go to a great studio with a great room and expensive mics and do it right. Get as much info as possible and then make the decisions at home.

Can you give one or two recommendations to other people who are getting into recording music at home?

Do the most with what you've got. Learn your equipment and make mistakes. Have fun with it and don't be too hard on yourself. If it's horrible, redo it differently. Learn to make decisions and stick by them. Trust your instincts. People want personality, not sonic perfection.

Can you give me your favourite recording anecdote?

There have been loads and loads of great moments. Recording horn sections in my guest bedroom, recording

>>

vocals through my answering machine or doing keyboard
arpeggios using my cell phone. But the biggest revelation
was realising that hey ... I can actually do this ... at
home!

Parameters

Samplers are classified into different groups, according to parameter capabilities. Some examples of these parameters are:

- Polyphony: how many audio tracks can be played at once
  through your sampler.
- Sample Space: how much memory is available on your
  sampler.
- Channels: how many different MIDI channels are available
  for different instruments.
- Bit depth: how much sample resolution can be supported.
- Outputs: how many audio outputs are available.

Examples of samplers include those made by AKAI – the MPC500,
MPC1000, MPC2000, MPC2000XL, MPC3000, MPC3000XL,
MPC3000LE, MPC4000 and the MPC60 – as well as those made
by Roland and the S series: S-10, S-50, S-330, S-550, S-760, S-770.

Software-based samplers

If you are on a budget and new to home recording, it might be
worth looking into software-based samplers. They're relatively
cheap (sometimes even free) and are fairly easy to use.

Recently, the huge increases in computer power and memory
have made it possible to develop software applications that

can produce the same level of performance and capability as the hardware-based units. Some believe that 'soft samplers' lack sample editing and sample recording capability, so aren't quite as good as their hardware counterparts. However, there are a few software-based samplers that provide sample editing and comprehensive effects, as well as the other functions expected from a sampler. Among them are Image-Line DirectWave, E-mu Emulator X, FL Studio, also called Fruity Loops Studio (described earlier) and TASCAM Gigastudio (originally Gigasampler).

Using samples – what kinds of samples are available to you?

Once recorded, samples can be edited, played back or looped – i.e. played back continuously. Types of samples include:

Loops

The drum and percussion parts of many modern recordings are really a variety of short samples of beats strung together. Many libraries of beats exist and are licensed so that the user incorporating the samples can distribute their recording without paying royalties. Such libraries can be loaded into samplers. Though percussion is a typical application of looping, many kinds of samples can be looped. A brief search online will provide you with software that specialises in creating loops.

Samples of musical instruments

Whereas loops are usually a phrase played on a musical instrument, this type of sample is usually a single note. Music workstations and samplers use samples of musical instruments as the basis of their own sounds, and are capable of playing a sample back at any pitch. Many modern synthesisers and drum machines also use samples as the basis of their sounds. Most samples are created in professional recording studios using world-class instruments played by accomplished musicians. These are usually developed by the manufacturer of the instrument or by a subcontractor who specialises in creating such samples. There are businesses and individuals who create libraries of samples of musical instruments. Of course, a sampler allows anyone to create such samples.

Samples of recordings

There are several genres of music in which it is commonplace for an artist to sample a phrase of a well-known recording and use it as an element in a new composition. Two well-known examples include the sample of Rick James's 'Super Freak' in MC Hammer's 'U Can't Touch This' and the sample of Queen and David Bowie's 'Under Pressure' in Vanilla Ice's 'Ice Ice Baby'. You will have to get permission to use such samples, and it is often extremely expensive, even if you get the all-clear.

Samples of spoken word

Usually taken from films or TV, spoken word samples are often used for humorous or atmospheric effect. For example, Goa trance often employs samples of people talking about drugs, spirituality or science fiction themes. Industrial is known for samples from horror/sci-fi movies, news broadcasts, propaganda reels and speeches by political figures (the band Ministry is notorious for sampling both the younger and elder George Bush).

Unconventional sounds

Some common examples include sirens and klaxons, locomotive whistles, gunshots, natural sounds such as whale song, and cooing babies. It is common in theatrical sound design to use this type of sampling to store sound effects that can then be triggered from a musical keyboard or other software. Some people have even been known to record the sound of animals, traffic or crowds. It's becoming increasingly popular to distinguish your music by the samples you create.

Tom Green

Tom Green (aka Another Fine Day) spent the 80s living in squats and contributing odd noises to locally issued 'dub plates' in Brixton, south London, and playing African music with London-based artists such as Abdul Tejan Jalloh. As the dance music scene picked up in the early 90s, Tom was asked by Alex Paterson to find ideas and sounds for a new project called The Orb, and subsequently contributed to five albums by the acknowledged pioneers of ambient house music. Along the way he also made two albums under the name Another Fine Day, the debut *Life Before Land* being voted third in the *Independent*'s 'Greatest Ambient Albums' chart of 2006. Both AFD albums were recorded entirely at home in a standard bedroom studio.

These days Tom is still recording and releasing work under the Another Fine Day moniker, as well as producing prodigious quantities of commissioned music for libraries such as BMG. His work also turns up regularly on the BBC, Channel 4 and RTE. He recently completed a sound-track for the movie *Botched*, to be released in late 2007 by Warners. Albums to be released in 2007 on Tom's own AnotherFineLabel include *Music for MRI Scanners* (an ambient commission) and a third Another Fine Day album.

Do you record music at home/ have you ever recorded music at home?
Yes, two albums released on indie labels, loads of library music, TV music and film music.

Can you explain what kind of music you make?
Generally, 'instrumental electronica' of all kinds, also ersatz versions of jazz, classical and other genres for commissions.

Do you mix and master your own records?
Yes, though mastering often takes place elsewhere for projects that can afford it. These days, mixing is done mostly 'in the box', though old-fashioned dub mixes still take place using a desk.

What equipment/software do you use to record music at home?
Mac running Logic, loads of outboard synths and FX as well as virtual orchestras.

How do you go about recording vocals at home?
Stick a mic up in the control room (the only room). It works fine.

>>

Do you use samples, or pre-recorded beats?

I use sample libraries for classical mock-ups, occasional sample percussion loops. No loops or sounds from other artists' material.

Can you explain any unusual recording techniques you have used to capture a particular sound?

All kinds of things, from messing with phase to radical eq-ing – I use a lot of very slowed-down, effected sounds, where I'll sample a sound not for what it sounds like at the time but for what it will sound like slowed down, reversed and with a ruthless filter knocking out huge chunks of frequencies.

Do you use any unconventional instruments, or take samples from 'the world around you' to use in your music?

I play thumb pianos (kalimba, mbira) and usually make sure something from the outside world gets into most tunes, from birdsong (subjected to the above treatments) to traffic sounds – just about anything sounds good when reduced to 'grains', looped, slowed down and chorused. Waveforms (even very, very short ones) from the natural world can always be used like any standard synth oscillator and usually sound more interesting. Percussion can be derived from anything, and I'm always raiding the kitchen. More difficult these days, but in the past I've constructed reverbs from 30-foot lengths of plastic pipe, with a speaker at one end and a mic at the other.

>>

Do you enjoy recording at home?

I love the time and freedom, in all senses, including financial. Even if the room isn't acoustically perfect, after a few years you soon learn what sounds good and what doesn't, and how your mixes will translate into the real world.

Do you think musicians/producers can generate album-quality material at home, or is it better to use a studio?

No problem – I've been doing it for seventeen years. Acoustic musicians and those who need live drum kits and Marshall stacks cranked to 11 may be better off in a proper studio.

Do you have a record/publishing deal? If so, who with?

I have had recording deals with both majors and indies, but for my own projects these days I do it myself. Publishing is handled by Ross Fitzsimons at Kaleidoscope Music/Notting Hill Music.

Can you give one or two recommendations to other people who are getting into recording music at home?

Make sure you don't annoy the neighbours ... Use the limitations to your advantage: you can't match what major studios can do, but they won't be able to put the time into finding that particular sound that may make or break a tune. You can, usually by thinking laterally.

Make sure your signal chain is matched throughout – there's no point buying an esoteric mic pre-amp if your

>>

>>

mic is rubbish, and vice versa. Don't buy the cheapest, but don't buy the really expensive stuff either, unless the rest of your monitoring and signal chain is already of pretty good quality.

Treat your room acoustically to get rid of the worst problems, but it's not really necessary to do the whole floating-floor thing unless you intend to make a very loud noise indeed. Even so, there's usually a minimum of treatment necessary which is always a better investment than expensive gear in an untreated room.

A favourite recording anecdote?

I once recorded a flute line for a well-known ambient dub act, back in the 90s. During the take, they set off a full-size smoke machine in the small control room. As I opened the door to go in and have a listen, a wall of smoke came out ... and I entered a dark room, full of smoke, giggles, and an engineer with his nose down on the desk trying to work out what the hell was going on. Apparently this was a deliberate attempt to upset the recording process, in that nobody could tell what fader or knob was which, and therefore all kinds of 'serendipitous wrongnesses' would turn up and make things more interesting. They could have just turned the lights out, but that wouldn't be half so much fun ... It must have worked, since the resulting album ended up at the top of the UK charts!

Plug-ins and effects

What are plug-ins?

Plug-ins are downloads available on the web which, when used in conjunction with your chosen recording software application, can change the sounds of your songs with special effects.

Just a few years ago, the term 'plug-in' didn't mean much to the average computer-based musician. These days no one can do without their plug-ins. But with what seems like about a million of them on the market, in freeware, shareware and commercial varieties, how can you know which ones are really the cream of the crop, other than by spending half your life downloading and auditioning demos? It's difficult to explain exactly what kind of sound a plug-in will make, but here's a list of some DIY artist's favourites.

Reverb: Audioease Altiverb/Logic/SIR Convolution Reverb

Reverb is the echoing sound that you will hear on pop vocals and sometimes guitar. Altiverb's sound is meant to be particularly clear and it's possible to try the reverb sound with a flick of a button, so you can experiment with it before saving. Another reverb plug-in recommended by those in the know is the SIR Convolution Reverb, available as a free download on the web.

Some suggest that Logic's built-in convolution reverb isn't bad at all. If you have fairly modest reverb requirements, you probably don't need to look any further.

Dynamics

These are effects that change the feel of your songs through limiting and compressing your audio tracks. Basically, it all refers to the volume of the various parts of your song. If a song is limited, the loudest spikes are removed; if it's compressed, it is further reduced. You may wish to limit your songs so they don't become distorted, which is possible when recording. There are various dynamic plug-ins that allow you to change the feel of a song:

PSP Audioware Vintage Warmer

In the age of digital, some people say that the 'warmth' of a song is lost in the digitisation process. The Audioware Vintage Warmer does what it says on the tin – it adds that analogue-sounding warmth to your songs, making them sound like records you would hear on the radio. One DIY artist said, 'Despite Vintage Warmer being one of the earliest distortion/warming plug-ins, PSP nailed the sound and it's a secret weapon for many recording fanatics.'

Waves Renaissance De-esser

The de-esser removes all of the hissing sounds in your recording, particularly the 'sss' sounds on your vocals. Many DIY artists swear by it.

Guitar Processor: Native Instruments Guitar Rig 2

Don't know how to play guitar? Then this plug-in might be for you. It allows you to create an authentic guitar sound by using a keyboard or even your computer's typepad.

Pitch Processor: Celemony Melodyne

For any type of sophisticated pitch correction, Melodyne is considered the bee's knees because it hands you so much corrective power via such a straightforward visual interface. Not only can it correct pitch in a more natural-sounding way than many of its competitors, but it also allows you to manipulate pitch slurs and to increase or decrease the amount of natural vibrato. You can even use it to lengthen or shorten existing notes or to drag notes to new pitches, to create believable harmony parts.

Those examples barely touch the surface of what is out there, but they do give you a good idea of what plug-ins can achieve. If you are confident enough to try more, a simple search on the web will provide you with more options.

Other effects
What is Flanging?
Flanging is a time-based **synthetic** sound which occurs when two identical MIDI signals are mixed together, but with one signal time-delayed by a small and gradually changing amount, usually smaller than 20 milliseconds. This produces a swept '**comb filter**' effect.

What are comb filters?
Comb filters have that name because of the way the sound appears graphically on the screen – like a comb with a series of regularly spaced spikes. In simple terms, the comb filter tool adds a delayed version of your sound on top of the original track you recorded. You will most likely have encountered the comb filter sound while listening to dance tracks – the trademark 'euphoric' climbing of a sound has been prevalent for the last fifteen years, if not longer. To learn more about filters such as these, refer to your software handbook.

Scott Doran – bass, vocals, Eskimo Disco

Eskimo Disco have been playing their infectious party music at warehouse parties, clubs and festivals across the UK, including supports with the Arctic Monkeys, The Rakes, The Subways, The Young Knives, Chromeo, Mint Royale and Jamie Liddell. 'One of the best live bands of the year,' says Playlouder.com. The band reached no. 15 in the charts in 2006 with their debut single '7–11'. The next single 'What Is Woman?', came out on the legendary Stiff Records on 14 May 2007. Their debut album was set to arrive in summer 2007.

Do you record music at home/ have you ever recorded music at home?
We record most of our music at home, and then take it in to the studio for a mixdown, use the big speakers for monitoring. Recording at home is a great way for musicians to get their ideas down without relying on producers (take the power back, I say).

Can you explain what kind of music you make?
Electro, pop, rock, dance, fuck punk, I think!

What equipment/software do you use to record music at home?
Logic, though I'm starting to get into Pro Tools – I think you get a wider sound.

How do you go about recording vocals at home?
Hunched over the computer at 3 a.m. with a beer.

How do you go about recording instruments/percussion at home?
We use loops for demos then get our drummer in the studio for the real thing.

Can you explain any unusual recording techniques you have used to capture a particular sound?
We layer up lots of keyboard, sometimes up to 70 layers in fact. We also record secret messages in the music to get our fans hooked.

Do you use any unconventional instruments, or take samples from 'the world around you' to use in your music?
We use vocoder in almost all our songs. What we really want is an actual robot in the band to sing with us. Maybe he could carry my bass amp too.

Do you enjoy recording at home? If so, what's so special about it?
Recording at home's great. You can spend hours going through hundreds of new sounds and really developing your sound.

Do you think musicians/producers can generate album-quality material at home, or is it better to use a studio?
I think software can do it but putting your music through a big SSL desk and pumping it will always give you a better album.

Do you have a record/publishing deal? If so, who with?
We're working with Stiff Records and are looking at a few publishing deals as we speak.

Can you give one or two recommendations to other people who are getting into recording music at home?
There are a lot of people making music at home these days but computers don't write songs, so to make yourself stand out, think about the song idea before you get carried away with tricks and sounds. And buy a Vintage Warmer compressor.

A favourite recording anecdote?
We recorded at Nellee Hooper's studio last year (he's got a cinema in there) and the last artist in there before us was P Diddy. Apparently he turned up for his session with an entourage of twenty girls, who are there to make him feel like a star when he's singing. We tried it when we recorded our album. It really works.

Mixing

Audio mixing is used in sound recording and audio editing to balance the relative volume and frequencies (sometimes known as dynamics) of the tracks recorded.

Each track you have laid down will be recorded at a different volume and frequency – say, one track for your vocals, another for guitar, another for drums and so on. In the mixing process, you will make decisions as to how all of these tracks will sit together in a song. It may be that you lower the volume of your drums, in order to highlight a louder guitar or vocal part. Or you may wish to start your song with a loud, crashing intro. Mixing will allow you to put the jigsaw of your song together, making sure that all of the separate parts sit well with each other.

You have undoubtedly encountered mixing before now. At every gig an engineer will mix the sound live from a desk situated at the back of the venue. You will have seen the dozens of tracks and knobs being pulled this way and back in order to achieve a perfect sound. Do not be alarmed! With the help of mixing software, there will be no need for you to get your head around enormous mixing desks.

Another example of mixing can be seen in nightclubs in every town in every country each night of the year. A professional DJ is a mixer extraordinaire, working all of the tracks together as he/she performs. It often makes for a fascinating sight to see how it's accomplished. If you know any DJs, you might want to watch them and learn some tricks.

A recent trend is mixing your tracks to 5.1 surround sound. Your software application should have the facility for you to switch your records to surround sound very easily indeed. Normally you will find it as an option in the mixing menu.

Equipment and software required

Audio mixing is becoming increasingly more popular on digital audio workstations and more and more artists are using software to mix their work. Sometimes you will find that you can mix your records using the software you have chosen to record your songs, such as Pro Tools, Audacity and Logic. In fact, Pro Tools is favoured by many home musicians for mixing. Alternatively, there are many basic applications available for mixing online, which often come with tutorials. In fact, it is possible to download free mixing applications, but as ever, you must watch that your download isn't going to arrive pre-installed with a load of random programs that will serve only to clog up your computer.

Examples of mixing software available on the web for download include: Power Mixer 2.1 (size: 491KB), sonicOne 1.1 (2293KB), OpenSebJ 0.1 (965KB), Amphiotik Synthesis 2.04 (14348K), CSMD 1.52 (2000K). Power Mixer is available for around £10–15, whereas the Amphiotik Synthesis 2.04 is quite expensive at £130–140.

Alternatively, you can use an audio mixing console, or mixing desk, as they are also known. However, unless you have spare cash and time on your hands to learn the artful technique of using one, it's probably best to let your computer and software do most of the job for you.

A mixing console has numerous rotating controls (potentiometers) and sliding controls (faders, which are also potentiometers). These are used to control volume, the addition of effects such as reverb, and the frequency (also known as equalisation) of audio signals. On most consoles, the controls that apply to a single channel of audio (that is to say, a bassline, or vocal etc) are arranged in a vertical column called a 'channel strip'. In professional studios you will see that consoles carry hundreds of channel strips.

Mixing consoles and phantom power

Phantom power is an electrical current that is transmitted over microphone cables. The standard current is +48v DC. It is called 'phantom' power because it is effectively invisible to balanced microphones. Phantom power is used to supply a voltage potential to condenser (or capacitor) microphones. It can also be used to supply current to active electronics found in dynamic and ribbon microphones or active DI boxes. Make sure you know if your dynamic or ribbon mic requires phantom power before engaging it, as you could damage a microphone not designed for it.

A phantom power supply will typically be built into mixing consoles, external pre-amps and computer audio interfaces.

You should switch phantom power off when connecting or disconnecting a line from the channel. It is also a good idea to mute the output of the channel or pre-amp before engaging phantom power as it can create a 'pop' that could damage your speakers or injure (or at the very least annoy) a musician or engineer wearing headphones.

When buying a mixing console, it is important to understand how phantom power is switched. Most professional or high-end gear will allow you to switch phantom power on or off on each individual channel.

Mixing with headphones

Some people have suggested that it is impossible to mix a song using headphones: after all, you surely need big loudspeakers to hear every tiny detail? This isn't necessarily true. Anyway, if you live in a house with other people, you simply won't be able to torment them with the same tracks or loops being played over and over again.

Here's a bit of science to explain how you interpret what you hear over loudspeakers and headphones. When listening to loudspeakers, your right ear receives sounds from the left channel as well as the right, but with a slight delay and reduced volume. This is due to the 'shadowing' effect of the head, and in particular the external parts of the ears, which act like complex direction-dependent tone controls. You also hear additional reflections from the room around you and its contents. On headphones, however, you obviously only hear the left channel in your left ear and the right in your right ear. Any hard-panned sounds will be heard through one ear, which sounds very unnatural.

When sounds panned to the middle (you will see this option in the waveform screen of your mixing software) are played through loudspeakers they are heard 'in front', but the same sounds on headphones appear to be emanating from inside your head. So, if you are mixing using headphones, it is possible that the final cut of your song may sound unbalanced.

A lot of stereo albums released before high-quality head-phones were popular, such as Beatles and early Pink Floyd LPs, and many releases from the 60s and 70s, almost sound wrong on headphones now, because the sound is coming at you from seemingly the wrong place.

Some headphone amps, accessories and plug-ins provide optional 'crossfeed' that mixes a little of the left-hand channel into the right and vice versa, to mimic the natural behaviour of our ears. This is sometimes known as acoustic simulation.

Just as with loudspeakers, different brands of headphones sound different, and you generally get what you pay for. However, you can find some excellent headphones for less than the price of a cheap pair of speakers, so it might be wise not to compromise. There are quite a few types of headphone available, and some are more suitable for mixing than others. Traditional headphones or 'cans' are more correctly termed circumaural devices, since they cover the outer ear, while the supra-aural type sit on top of the ears. Both are available in open and closed varieties.

Nevertheless, for mixing, the majority of recommended models tend to be open-backed (for comfort and cool ears over long periods) and circumaural (for the deepest and most natural bass end). Sennheiser's HD650s (£180) (www.sennheiser.co.uk) are very highly regarded for their detailed yet neutral sound and for their bass extension, as well as the Grado RS2s (£150) for intricate details, while others say that AKG's K701s (£220+) (www.akg-acoustics.com) have the cleanest sound of all. Bear in mind that some effects applied to your tracks might not work on headphones, for example, 3D placement plug-ins that are designed for use with loudspeakers. The converse applies too.

It is possible to mix through headphones, but it is wise to listen to the song from time to time through all different kinds of speakers, both at home and even in the car, as it will give you a better understanding of how other people will hear your songs. And remember, most people these days are listening through computers or iPod headphones, so you have a certain licence not to make the mix absolutely perfect!

Jimmy Behan – musician/ producer/DJ

Born in Carlow, Ireland, Jimmy moved to Dublin in the early 90s and studied sound engineering at Pulse Recording College. He released his first EP on Kin Recordings in 2001, followed by a split seven-inch on Road Relish. His debut album *Days Are What We Live In* was released on Elusive Recordings in 2004. He's supported, among others, Lali Puna, Four Tet, Murcof, Manitoba and Blue States, and has had numerous appearances at Dublin's Lazybird and Ballroom of Romance nights, the MOR festival 2004 and the Big Chill festival in the UK in 2002 and 2005. He was awarded an MPhil in Music and Media Technologies from Trinity College, Dublin in 2006.

Do you record music at home/ have you ever recorded music at home?
I do almost everything at home.

Can you explain what kind of music you make?
I suppose you would call it electronic music, though it incorporates a lot of acoustic sounds also. Most of it is instrumental.

>>

>>

Do you mix and master your own records?

I mix them as best I can while trying the mixes out on a range of different systems. Ideally I'd like to use a mix engineer in a proper studio but that's not always possible. It's often useful to have a fresh pair of ears to help with the mix. I wouldn't attempt to master them for release as my monitoring set-up just wouldn't be accurate enough. I might try and master something with a less busy mix, like an ambient or abstract piece, where radio or club play isn't really a consideration. A good mastering engineer will ensure a good result across a range of systems. It's just too important a stage to leave to chance.

What equipment/software do you use to record music at home?

Software:

- Steinberg's Cubase SX3
- a program called Audiomulch developed by Ross Bencina
- Cycling '74's MaxMsp
- Steinberg's Wavelab 5
- Native Instruments' Kontakt soft-sampler and Akoustik Piano
- some audio-to-Midi converters
- a few soft-synths
- a variety of Vst plug-ins

Hardware:

- Dell PC with M-Audio Audiophile 2496 sound card

>>

- Acer laptop with Echo Indigo sound card
- Soundcraft Compact10 mixer
- Tannoy Reveal monitors
- Samson Servo 170 monitor amp
- Yamaha CS1x midi keyboard
- Røde NT-1A condenser mic

How do you mix and master your own records?

I like to spend a long time on a mix, tweaking it and coming back to it. I'll never do a mix in one sitting. You're emotional and physical state at the time will impact on the result. You might mix something in the morning quite differently to how you might mix it at the end of the day and it's important to be aware of this. Trying it out on different playback systems is also important. Try it out on a domestic hi-fi system, headphones, car stereo, PA system if possible. You're looking for something that will work sufficiently on all these and more. I think it's better to leave something a little less mixed than over-cooking it and hoping the mastering engineer will fix it. I use Wavelab and Waves plug-ins if I'm trying to master something myself.

How do you go about recording vocals at home?

When I have done, which isn't often, I'll just try and minimise any noise and reflections in the room, use a decent condenser mic and a pop-shield and hope the alarm across the street doesn't go off! I might use some compression to get a better signal-to-noise ratio going

>>

into the sound card, but prefer to record it dry, so you have the choice of compressing after if need be. An over-compressed vocal can be hard to fix.

How do you go about recording instruments/percussion at home?
I don't often record instruments at home unless it's a guitar plugged straight in the mixer. I just don't have the space.

Do you use samples, or pre-recorded beats?
A mixture of both. I've a large library of the more generic sounds like kick, snare, tome etc. More recently I've been recording my own percussion sounds if I'm looking for something more unique. I rarely sample records any more though I used to a lot. I think this was a result of moving from using an Akai sampler for everything to using a decent DAW system. I'm processing and manipulating sounds a lot more now so I don't need as many sounds to begin with. Many of my earlier pieces were basically sample collages which were more beat-orientated, whereas now they feature more processing and manipulation of both sounds and Midi files. I'm also a bit more careful about the legalities of sampling than I used to be.

Can you explain any unusual recording techniques you have used to capture a particular sound?
I recently recorded some nice kick sounds using a contact mic attached to my mouse pad while tapping it with a pen.

>>

Do you use any unconventional instruments, or take samples from 'the world around you' to use in your music?

I use quite a few found sounds in my music by just recording things with the mic. I don't have a roomful of strange instruments, however. I do like things like thumb pianos and toy xylophones but I find once you use them, they're often left gathering dust on a shelf. I like recording sound spaces, which is something I want to do more of. Ironically, the pure, clean slate digital recording has offered in recent years has seen a greater awareness in many people's work in this area. Noise and texture are used as creative elements more readily than before. It's interesting to hear how people often feel a CD reissue will have less of an emotional impact than their original vinyl copy.

Do you enjoy recording at home? If so, what's so special about it?

I like the independence of it. I'm not relying on anyone else. It's obviously very convenient too. I like being in my own space both literally and creatively; it just feels more personal to me. I can work at my own pace too and take breaks when I want. You feel less pressure to always come out with something at the end of the day as you're not paying for studio time. There is a whole psychology going on as well, however, which you need to be aware of. There are times when you just feel entombed in this little world which can affect you in different ways, both good and bad.

>>

>>

Do you think musicians/producers can generate album-quality material at home, or is it better to use a studio?
It depends on what kind of music it is and what it's going to be used for. Obviously it suits the kind of music I make which doesn't utilise as much live recording as your average rock band, for example. So long as you're aware of the limits you can work within them. With a little care and attention, good results can be achieved. If the aesthetic of the music can complement the production, then even better. I think where most home-based set-ups fall down is in the monitoring. It's very difficult to mix or master with a monitoring environment that's just not accurate.

Can you give one or two recommendations to other people who are getting into recording music at home?
I think you've got to be prepared to give it a few years and always be aware of the limits you're working under. Spend money on the key elements of the audio chain like a good sound card, decent cabling, a good mic and good monitors. It's always worth looking into how you can improve your monitoring arrangement by minimising reflections and standing waves. I also think it's best to master a few pieces of software or hardware rather than having just a cursory knowledge of many. Use your limits creatively by maybe incorporating them into the aesthetic of the music. At the end of the day, the listener is more likely to react on an emotional level, so if the music is lacking there, no studio in the world will save you.

Mastering

Mastering is the process of preparing and transferring recorded audio from a source containing the final mix (see page 153) to a data storage device (the master). This is the source file from which all copies will be produced. It is the final stage at which you can make your recording sound as good as possible. Tasks such as editing, pre-gapping, levelling, fading in and out, noise reduction and other signal restoration and enhancement processes can be applied as part of the mastering stage. Your music is also put in its proper order at this stage – the actual running order of the tracks on an album. This is commonly called the assembly. The mastering process will differ according to what you want your final format to be – CD, vinyl, MP3. Each of these will be mastered in a different way, with different settings. The software you will be using will be preset with the different settings and you will be required to make a decision on the eventual format at that stage.

Mastering with digital technology

In the 1990s, old-fashioned mastering techniques were largely superseded by digital technology, with digital recordings now transferred to digital masters by an optical etching process that uses laser technology. That isn't to say that some studios don't still use the old tools – they do, and there are people who actually prefer to use the analogue process. Some engineers believe that this is still the best way to master your records. However, it's possible for you to use your computer and software to at least attempt the process of mastering. Some of those interviewed in this book suggest that you can make a professional-sounding master at home, while others avoid the laborious process altogether, leaving it to the experts.

The process of mastering an audio recording varies depending on what your song requires. Steps in the process typically include (but are not restricted to):

- Most of your audio will at this stage be on your computer, so open it in your chosen software – most packages come with a mastering facility (see the list below).
- Choose the order of your songs as they will appear on the album. Create, and decide the length of, the space between each track.
- Process the audio to maximise the sound quality for the medium on which the track will appear (for example, MP3). This isn't as easy as it sounds. The actual process which you will be taken through can be tricky, so it may be wise to read up about the subject, or even take a specialist mastering course. This might include: adjusting volumes, editing minor flaws, applying noise reduction to eliminate hum and hiss, dynamic compression, dynamic expansion, equalising audio between tracks.
- Move the track to the final format. Make sure to decide on the format of your track before you transfer: will it be made for audio CD, high-quality MP3, or even an AAC file so that it's compatible with iTunes?

These are just some pointers. Each situation will be different and it's entirely up to you to make a decision about how to approach it. There are no rules when it comes to recording in your own studio.

Examples of audio mastering plug-ins:

- Adobe Audition
- Apple WaveBurner
- Ardour
- Audio Cube
- BIAS Peak
- Cakewalk Sonar
- Cubase
- Digital Performer
- iZotope Ozone
- Nuendo
- Pro Tools
- PYRAMIX Virtual Studio
- SaDiE
- Sequoia
- Sonic Solutions
- Sonic Studio
- Sony CD Architect
- Sony Sonoma
- Sound Forge
- WaveLab
- XO Wave

Alasdair Reid

Originally from Edinburgh, Alasdair got into music through drumming. However, three years of music college, quickly followed by three stints drumming with bands that all were dropped by their record labels (usually within weeks of him joining), soon convinced him that 'staring at a singer's backside for a living' was not going to work out for him. Initial attempts at writing for short films (*The Ring* and *Phillip's Flashing Finger*) met with some success and led to work for Channel 4. To date, he has worked on a huge variety of films, programmes and commercials, including three BAFTA nominees and some compositions that have gone on to win awards both at home and abroad. His concert music has featured in several recitals at the Royal Festival Hall in London and he recently won the Volkswagen Score Prize at the 2006 Berlin Film Festival.

Do you record music at home/ have you ever recorded music at home? If so, what? Demos/finished singles/ finished albums?

I write and record music for TV and film at home – so stuff will begin as demos and eventually turn into finished masters to be dubbed to the project.

Can you explain what kind of music you make?

Given the nature of 'media' music, it's a pretty eclectic mix – everything from full orchestral pieces to thrash metal tracks, ten-second stings and commercials to sixty-minute soundtracks to a film.

What equipment/software do you use to record music at home?

I'm running Logic Pro7 on a Apple G5, which I use to

sequence and record all my music. My audio interface is an Apogee Ensemble, monitors are Adam S3a, a DAV BG-1 stereo preamp to record 'live' sources with (using an AKG c-414 B-ULS mic). A shed-load of software makes my job possible: the VSL Orchestral Library allows me to create convincing mock-ups of classical music, Altiverb (a reverb simulator) is unbeatable for reverb, and EQ / Dynamics / FX plug-ins from Sony Oxford, PSP Audioware, URS, SoundToys and Elemental Audio all make everything sound nice. The least sexy but most important piece of equipment has to be the acoustic treatment on the walls of my studio which goes a long way to controlling the echoes and nasty frequency anomalies inherent in any room. Without it, mixing would be very hit and miss.

Do you mix and master your own records? If so, how?
Yes, although you could argue that almost none of my work has a 'life' outside the film or programme it's written to accompany, so there are no records or CDs to be released.

Anyhow, I get everything up and running in Logic, get a balance that works on my main Adam monitors and then listen to it through a variety of sources – cheap and nasty speakers, car hi-fi, TV, anything. The idea being that a good mix will translate well to the listener in any listening environment. I keep tweaking the mix until it sounds good just about anywhere.

Mastering is something I'd prefer to leave to someone else, but in TV-land you often don't have time because of deadlines. So I use four excellent plug-ins to get me home: PSP's Master Compressor and Neon HR EQ, Sony's Inflator and Elemental Audio's Inspector XL. If I can't get a pleasing result with them, then I need to give up.

How do you go about recording instruments/percussion at home?

I'll use a variety of rooms in the house to record. The bathroom has a great sound that certainly isn't good but *is* interesting. Often, interesting is more important than good in my book. For more conventional sessions, I'll record in my studio — the background noise from my equipment is minimal, so it's possible to get a good sound, due to the acoustic treatment on the walls.

I was taught that good mic placement avoids a lot of mixing 'repair' work later on, so I'lll spend time finding the best micing position for the instrument I'm recording and then go from there.

Do you use samples, or pre-recorded beats?

Yes — almost everything I write is based around samples of one kind or another, whether it's an orchestral sound library or just a snatch of sound to be mangled with some software. Stylus RMX is a great 'instant' beat machine, but I'll always try and chop whatever it's producing up, so as not to fall into the trap of just using the same presets as the rest of the world. It only takes a minute or two, and makes all the difference.

>>

Can you explain any unusual recording techniques you have used to capture a particular sound?
Sticking your sound source at one end of a piece of piping (say 3 to 10ft long) and your mic at the other always guarantees a different sound, particularly for wind and brass instruments. And recently I've been experimenting with swinging a mic around in a big circle by its lead whilst recording an instrument or sound – the results are mixed, but when it works, it's great. The volume, tone and sense of space all change at the same time and you get an effect that'd be very hard to create using a computer or hardware FX box.

Do you use any unconventional instruments, or take samples from 'the world around you' to use in your music?
The real world is a great source of material – mainly because it has a rawness not found in a lot of synths or sample libraries. Favourite things include a big metal salad bowl from Ikea – hit in the right way it has a natural pitch bend to its metallic sound, which sounds huge once treated with reverb or echo. I'lll often 'play' drums using my fingers on the back of an acoustic guitar. The result is a wonderfully warm and natural sound that doesn't stand out as aggressively as a real kit would. For 'woosh' FX, nothing beats your own voice, heavily processed with delay, reverb and some sort of modulation – in an instant you can have wonderfully expressive and

nimble sound effects that would take hours to achieve with a synth.

Do you enjoy recording at home?
The downside is not being able to make as much noise as you like, whenever you like. Also, it's hard to achieve a truly quiet recording, unless you're willing to turn one room of your house into a padded cell ... But the best thing about recording at home is the lack of time vs. money constraints – the clock is not ticking! And it's only a short distance from the studio to falling into bed at 3 a.m.

Do you think musicians/producers can generate album-quality material at home, or is it better to use a studio?
They can, it's just a lot more work. And given that one person's album quality is another's dog-eared mess, it's difficult to make any kind of distinction. A lot of people record at home in studios that they've poured tens of thousands of pounds into, which poses the question 'Is it a home studio or a studio in a home?' If the budget is there, I always prefer to record critical parts in a well-equipped studio – things like vocals, live kit, solo instruments. It's always good to have an experienced engineer taking responsibility for your tracks and often the studio will be using equipment that I would have no chance of knowing how to use optimally, let alone afford.

Can you give one or two recommendations to other people who are getting into recording music at home?
Acoustic treatment: It is the most important thing in any recording or mixing environment – and because it's so unsexy, it's the thing most often ignored. If you're working in a room that doesn't allow you to hear your work accurately, due to room modes, standing waves, etc., then it doesn't matter how much money you've poured into gear. It'll end up sounding crap – or, at best, flawed. It doesn't cost a lot, and will never break down. Spend money on acoustic treatment before anything else. And wherever possible, buy the best equipment you can reasonably afford – it took me years to work out that I had spent a lot of money on cheap, inadequate gear only to get rid of it later at a huge loss, because it wasn't giving me the results I wanted. Good gear gives good results and holds its value almost indefinitely – it makes sense in the long run.

Tell us your favourite recording anecdote.
A friend was very excited when he bought his first pro microphone (a Røde NTK) – but he was a bit disappointed with the results he was getting. A couple of months after buying it he took it back to the music store to ask for a replacement. The shop checked it over and reported that it was fine. Not convinced, my mate grabbed the mic and started singing into it – 'Look, it sounds terrible!' It was only then that the shop staff realised the problem – for

>>

two months my friend had been singing into the top of a side-addressed mic...

(OK, I know – hardly a laugh a minute ... this story is only remotely funny if you already know the difference between a 'stage mic' (say an SM58, which you sing into the top of) and a side-address mic, kind of like the ones you see all the old-time crooners singing into.)

4

Now you have recorded a song, what are you going to do with it?

Record labels

Back in the day, record labels would have been your first port of call, maybe with the hope of trying to get the attention of an A&R scout or person, who would listen to your demo, come and see your gig and sign you to a multi-million-pound recording contract. This is no longer necessary, or even the best option. You may have noticed that the music industry is in freefall and, quite often these days, doesn't know if it's coming or going, what with the increase in DIY artists and the ongoing loss of sales – whether that be down to illegal file-sharing or plain terrible business management, which is more likely the case.

If you are determined to get a record deal, there are some things you should bear in mind first. Be careful to send your demo – which ought to be in MP3 format these days – to the right label. It's no good pitching folk music to a pop label, or rock music to a dance label. Do your research and target the record labels you think will like your music. Also, don't just aim for the big labels, of which there are currently four: SonyBMG, Warner Music, Universal and EMI. They are all in a right state at the moment and it's likely that, if you are signed, but don't sell adequately in your first year or two, you're going to be dropped at some point, which will involve legal costs, management companies and you forfeiting any type of advance you're on. It might be wise to look at small, independent labels, who will cut you a more sensible deal and, more often than not, are a lot more forward-thinking when it comes to releasing your material. Anyhow, you're a DIY artist, which means that you can get your music out there without the need for a record label anyway.

Using the web to make your music heard

177

Now you have recorded a song, what are you going to do with it?

Nizlopi, Koopa, Sandi Thom, The Feeling, Arctic Monkeys, Lily Allen and just about every musician who has ever heard of MySpace are now using the web to get their music out there.

With the advent of social networking sites, download sites for unsigned musicians, YouTube and other video-sharing sites, iTunes and Napster, it is now possible for musicians to side-step the big guys and distribute their own music (whether that be at a price or not) to anyone and everyone who might want to hear it, without the help (or hindrance) of a big record label.

These are amazing times. You can easily record a track, even make a video, write yourself a biography and organise a photo shoot and have all of that information up on the web for people to see in a flash and there is a raft of online services which will help you do exactly that. Again, don't be put off by the thought that it's all just too technical. It's easy and everything has been designed to make the process as pain-free as possible.

One of the best ways to learn how to promote your music online is to look at how acts that you like have promoted themselves using the web. You can pick up a lot of tips that way. The main thing is that you are creative and use the technology that is now available to your advantage. Who knows? You could be making cash and playing gigs before you know it.

MySpace
www.myspace.com

Although it's no secret and you probably have a page already, one of the best starting places is MySpace. The community website (now owned by the Fox Corporation) allows you to create your own artist page, upload up to four songs for people to listen to, send round bulletins advertising your songs and potential gigs and so on, as well as networking with other people on the service and building your fanbase. It's surprising how many artists are on MySpace, and it's a regular destination for labels looking for new material. One tip, however: make sure your page is as individual and uncluttered as possible. You want to show off your material, but not overwhelm people with too much information. Also, MySpace will soon be introducing the facility for you to sell your songs via the service, so this might be an option if you want to start generating a profit from the music you make.

Beware that garnering a million friends on MySpace does not translate into either being able to sell a lot of music or eventually stumbling upon a record deal. It has fast become transparent that people will bulk up their figures with anyone – it does not mean they're genuine fans or that they will buy your records. People are getting used to picking up music for free and it's up to you to use MySpace wisely as a marketing tool.

Garageband
www.garageband.com

(This Garageband is not to be confused with the software application GarageBand which we have covered elsewhere in this book.) Unlike MySpace, Garageband is a community website directly targeted at musicians from all over the world. In common with MySpace, it allows you to create a page dedicated to your music and upload a series of MP3s, but it is much, much more.

Firstly, you can sell your music through Garageband – setting the price at as little or as much as you want. The site and its owners will also help you sell tickets for your gigs and any affili- ated merchandise (T-shirts, artwork, posters and so on). Also, members of the site get to preview your music and review it — their reviews count towards a Garageband chart.

The site also has a deal with 400 radio stations in the US, which regularly play tracks featured on Garageband. Once you have uploaded your songs, you can also submit them for consideration.

My Bedroom Studio
www.mybedroomstudio.com/profile/
emasters

As all record labels now scout around for music online, it comes as no surprise that there is a website dedicated to the unsigned, home musician. My Bedroom Studio, which is owned by EMasters, contains everything you would expect on a music-based social networking site: videos, member profiles where you can upload music, and a user forum for swapping ideas. EMasters also owns another website, www.emasters.co.uk, where you can have your tracks mastered by a professional (the site says they use some of the best producers in the world, but that is probably debat- able!). You upload your songs at a cost and they are returned, via an FTP download site, within a given timeframe. The first three songs are free and the price differs from there onwards.

Those three websites are free. It differs from here onwards.

IndieStore
www.indiestore.co.uk

One of the most sophisticated tools for a DIY artist on the web,

IndieStore allows you to plug your tracks into its aggregation service, which supplies music to all online retailers, whether big guys like iTunes or a local record shop that has an online download store. IndieStore offers two packages to DIY artists – a free, basic package and for a price, IndieStore Pro. Here's a brief rundown of what both can do for you:

IndieStore Starter is the free service level for artists just getting into the digital music revolution. The Starter features will warm you up to creating your artist presence online. Features include:

- 70 per cent revenue share on all tracks sold
- up to four track uploads
- multi-format downloads – no digital rights management
- free tracks
- pre-orders – organise for your song to be ordered in advance of release (as you would with Amazon)
- choice of taking the IndieStore web address (URL) or setting up one up of your own
- blog, gallery, events calendar facilities
- user-ratings and comments
- real-time reporting
- monthly accounting
- PayPal and Click & Buy payments
- IndieStore flashplayer for videos
- Last.fm – your music played & sold on Last.fm

IndieStore Pro includes enhanced features, such as:
- 80 per cent revenue share on all tracks sold
- chart eligibility in the UK, US and more than twenty other

181

Now you have recorded a song, what are you going to do with it?

countries – if you sell enough, your songs can be included in the charts
- ISRC generation and registration – information that will allow you to register your song for the charts
- up to 20 track uploads – you can put entire albums online
- music synchronisation – IndieStore is also used by advertising agencies to source music for TV and radio ads. If your track is selected you will earn 80 per cent of the licensing fee paid.
- monthly accounting – you can earn cash on a monthly basis – the lowest minimum balance must be £25 before you are paid
- advanced styling options on your pages
- plus the same features as listed in the free service

Julie Thompson

Julie is a songer-songwriter signed to Reverb. As part of a duo called Elektralow, she released an self-financed album in 2004. She has written and toured with a number of performers including Freestylers, James Holden and DJ Tiesto, as well as penning hits for pop artists such as Kym Marsh. In 2007 she wrote and produced singles released on Tiesto's label.

What have you recorded at home?
In excess, I'd say, of more than 500 songs over the course of the last eight years: both my own compositions, co-

writes with other people and vocals on tracks which are sent to me by other artists and producers.

Can you explain what kind of music you make?
It's all different: from pop record pitches to record labels to fully produced vocals for dance tracks.

Do you mix and master your own records from home?
No, I take my tracks to friends who work at studios for that.

What equipment and software do you use?
An Apple Mac G5, Pro Tools LE with an M Box, a Røde NT2 microphone, a Roland XP50 keyboard and plug-ins for native piano sounds – my favourite is Akoustic's piano plug-in. I had a terrible problem with latency when I used my G4 with Pro Tools and the M Box. I think the problem was with the M Box itself, so now quite often I will record instruments through Logic and edit using Pro Tools. I much prefer editing with that than anything else.

How do you record vocals?
I use a pop shield. Before I had money to spend, I used a pair of tights over a coat hanger for a pop shield, which can be almost as effective – in fact, I recorded my vocals for the Holden and Thompson tracks using that and they went on to be played on the radio and in clubs! I'll sometimes create a vocal 'den' using duvets and blankets, which cuts out external noise and makes my vocals warmer, and sometimes it really does make a difference where you posi-

tion the mic in the room. Most of the time I will record my vocals section by section – so a verse a time, or a chorus at a time – then I will 'comp' (compile: pick out the best sections and piece them together in editing) to make the final cut. One of my editing tricks is to pan my vocals, so that the main vocal comes through the middle, but other vocal tracks come out of the left and right speakers. It gives that all-encompassing, dreamy and close sound.

Do you use any other techniques?
Sometimes I find reversing a melody helps me to come up with ideas when I'm working on a song – I have a reverse plug-in to do that. I know some people who double-track vocals and then compress them to get rid of the harsh sounds of certain syllables and then layer them over a pure, untreated vocal track.

Do you enjoy recording at home?
Yes, it is much better than being in a studio. There are things I will try at home that I don't like trying in front of other people. And you can stop for cups of tea.

Do you think you can generate studio sound quality at home?
Yes, but sometimes when I hand over my tracks for mixing I feel as though it might have been better to record them in a vocal booth, so it's easier for them. It's really good to try and keep vocals as clean as possible, especially when you are sending them into a studio for mixing.

>>

Do you have a record/publishing deal?

I have an arrangement with a publishing company called Reverb, who also manage me. I tend to only work with people who have publishing deals, since those are the people that Reverb put me in touch with.

Do you have any tips for people recording music at home?

If you record a bad song, it doesn't matter how much you fiddle with it in the studio, it will always be a bad song. Make sure that the song sounds good on an acoustic guitar – no amount of tampering will ever improve a bad song.

Any amusing anecdotes?

There was one time I was in the studio, watching an Indian girl record a song. Indian songs are sung in quarter tones so, for example, they will hit the note between C and C sharp – it's not a technique you will hear in western music. The final track was left with an engineer who had just started his training and he thought he should autotune the vocals. This meant that he deleted all of the quarter tones and the entire beauty of her voice was lost. He tried to make it sound like Kylie – it was hilarious!

Last.fm
www.last.fm

Last.fm is one of the big success stories of the digital revolution. If you're not familiar with it already, it is basically a recommendation service. The idea is that you can type in the names of your favourite bands and Last.fm will deliver a set of results containing music that sounds similar to the acts you like. Each band or artist has its own page on Last.fm, with functionality to buy music, options to join forums to chat to other fans of that music, and a wealth of radio stations based on your favourite genre.

What is little known, however, is that you can also use it to build a fanbase for your music. DIY artists are encouraged to promote their music on Last.fm, because the filtering and recommendation features mean that the music will be played for users who already like similar artists. You can upload your own music for streaming and Last.fm provides access to weekly airplay statistics, with facilities for promoting individual tracks. You may also choose whether your music is to be made available for streaming only, or for purchase or free download.

Once you have had a track or tracks 'scrobbled' by at least one user (i.e. included on a list of tracks they like and uploaded to the service), Last.fm automatically generates a main artist page, even if there is no music available for streaming on the radio. This page shows details of the total number of plays, the total number of listeners, the most popular weekly and overall tracks, the top weekly listeners, linked groups and journals, a list of similar artists, most popular tags and a shoutbox for messages. There are also links to events, additional album and individual track pages and similar artists' radio. If the artist has music available for streaming or download, an embedded flashplayer is also included with samples of the most popular tracks.

Users may add relevant biographical details and other information to any artist's main page in the form of a Wiki. Edits are regularly moderated to prevent vandalism. A photograph of the artist may also be added. If more than one is submitted, the most popular is chosen by public vote.

Artists-First.Net
www.artists-first.net

Artists-First is an online resource that allows you to sell your music for a small transactional cost of 5 per cent on every track sold through the company's main website. The website gives you the tools to achieve many things. Simply by signing up with an account, the owners of the site – who have been doing this since the turn of the millennium – encode your music (that is, make sure it's available as the right digital format – all you have to do is supply a good quality MP3), upload the tracks, price them correctly (according to what you specify), make them chart-eligible, re-encode them so they can be sold through mobile phones, and deliver physical products – that is, CDs, anywhere in the world – to your fans, while you make five times the money you would earn on iTunes. Sound too good to be true? It isn't. Selling directly through Artists-First means you can start to give fans what they want, when they want. Once something is recorded (live or in the studio) you should be offering it for sale immediately. It would take at least six weeks to get a song on iTunes and often 5 weeks, 6 days, 23 hours and 59 minutes is way too long! No doubt you'll be so excited, you'll want to get your music out there immediately. Artists-First lets you do exactly that.

The owners – most of whom are musicians themselves – are also introducing a facility this year whereby any advertising revenue generated on your online page (which will be hosted by the company) will be directed back to you too. You can also ask for your music to be sold as ringtones – yet another way of making some cash quickly. There are no charges for applying to be sold on Artists-First, and no setup fees, licence fees, storage limits or any other costs. The only time you pay is when you sell something and then it's only 5 per cent. You've nothing to lose!

Digital download services and aggregators

There are more and more download stores appearing on the web. As well as iTunes, Napster, Rhapsody (US), Virgin Megastore, HMV and even brands such as Coke are giving away downloads. It is possible to make your music available on these services through digital aggregators. There is no point in contacting them directly since they are overwhelmed with songs on a daily basis. Digital aggregators include companies like AWAL (UK and Europe), who are able to get tracks on iTunes, 7Digital (UK and Europe), Ioda (Europe) and The Orchard (US). What you might find, however, is that these companies are becoming more in demand and may charge you for the service. Also, never sign an exclusive agreement with just one company – you want to exploit as many routes as you can.

Podcasting and synchronisation

After the success of Ricky Gervais' and Russell Brand's podcasts in the UK, chances are you know how these work anyway. If you don't, here's a brief overview.

A podcast is a digital media file, or a series of digital files, distributed over the web using syndication feeds, for playback on portable media players and home computers. When you sign up to a podcast you are basically opening your computer to automatically receive a piece of data over the web at a specific time. At the moment, licensing issues are preventing bands and artists from using podcasts successfully – there are too many people who want to be paid for the rights to broadcast music in this fashion, and there's a bit of a lock down. However, this can work in your favour. Putting together a few tracks and making them available over a given period of time can help to build a buzz about your music. The only catch is, you need a web page to make your podcast available. For that, you can use a blog (see below).

Synchronisation has grown to be a thriving scene for DIY artists, with many songs being picked up for use in advertisements or films. Getting yourself a list of advertising companies and finding out who's in their music departments might be a wise choice. It doesn't take long to fire off an email with an MP3 attached. There are also a raft of companies scouring around for music for films and adverts – a search on the web should provide some useful sources of contacts.

Blogs

The blogs (short for weblog) has been around for some time now. Blogs enable you to create a page on the web, which can be updated with an easy-to-use interface and include material such as video, audio and pictures. Companies that give away blog creation software on the web include eBlogger, Moveable Type, SixApart, Wordpress and Windows Live Writer. These are only a handful of examples, so look on the web for more.

As a DIY artist, you're going to need to use a blogging software company that will also host MP3s, so people can download your music or stream it. This might be at a small charge to you, but it won't be extortionate, or at least it shouldn't be. Blogging has become very fashionable recently, and even the major record labels have jumped on board: SonyBMG has two blogs (columbiademos.co.uk and rcademos.co.uk) where you can upload your demos or even finished songs for people at the label to hear.

Bear in mind with blogs that you are not going to get any attention simply by putting one live on the web, and you will not be able to sell material through them. They are just one of the marketing tools available to you; you will also need to promote your music in forums, on other blogs and through community websites such as MySpace or Facebook to get noticed. However, blogs can work very well in tandem with any of the other services we have mentioned above.

Oisin Lunny

From a background of over seventeen years in the music business, Oisin Lunny is now composing and producing music for film, TV and radio and online with his own company, Lifeblood Productions. In the past two years the Hove-based composer and producer (and son of Donal Lunny, featured elsewhere in this book) has composed and produced the ident music for the Irish terrestrial TV station RTE ONE with his father, and written original

>>

music for the feature films *I Want Candy* and *The Waiting Room*. He has produced sync music for a Sky Broadband TV advert, the film *Derailed* starring Jennifer Aniston and Clive Owen, a Northern Bank TV advert and BBC 1's Children in Need. Over the course of his career Oisin has also released records on Talkin' Loud, Pussyfoot, More Rockers and Independiente and signed publishing deals with Warner Chappell, Island Music and Seeca. He has also toured with Depeche Mode and U2 and worked with Bono & Adam Clayton, Shara Nelson, DJ Premier, Beth Orton and Sinead O'Connor.

Do you record music at home?
Yes – almost everything has been recorded at home with a couple of exceptions. Some of the tracks for the 2000 Independiente release *When It Hits You Feel No Pain* were mixed in my home studio, likewise most film and TV commissions I have been involved with.

Can you explain what kind of music you make?
It's a mixture of live and electronic elements drawing from a wide variety of influences: techno, hip hop, northern soul, ambient etc.

Music for film and TV is written to order with a orchestral or more contemporary feel as required.

Do you mix and master your own records?
Mostly – but for bigger commissions I prefer to get someone else to master. I've been lucky enough to work

with some really talented mastering engineers in the past, such as Paul Solomon. A good master can elevate your recordings onto another level, particularly in terms of dancefloor or radio impact.

How do you go about mixing your own records?

It's a gradual process – often with electronic music the arrangement of the elements plays a large part in the overall sound, so mixing can be part of the writing process from early on. In terms of media commissions I will do a rough mix directly on my Mac using Logic, and if the client likes the ideas, I'll go on to separate the individual elements across the 42 input channels of the O2R and mix from there, applying compression, EQ and additional effects from the O2R or increasingly from Logic. The built-in effects in Logic are very useful – Space Designer is a particular favourite, but you can get some amazing free plug-ins such as Ohm Force Camel Crusher. There are some pretty good freeware virtual instruments out there as well such as AUTOMAT, Crystal and Remedy – www.kvraudio.com is the best source of plug-in information online.

What equipment/software do you use to record music at home?

- 17" Mac Book Pro running Logic 7 Pro, Reason, Absynth, Garritan Personal Orchestra, Korg Digital Edition, GarageBand and more
- Roland JP8000, Casio CZ3000, EMU SP1200, Procussion, Yamaha TX81z, Quasimidi 309, Microwave XT

- RME Fireface 800
- Yamaha 02R
- Fender guitar & bass

How do you go about recording vocals at home?
A Røde NT2 is plugged into the mic pre-amp of the
Fireface 800 and positioned close to the vocalist.

**How do you go about recording instruments/percussion
at home?**
In general I plug directly in to the RME Fireface, but with
some acoustic instruments, recorded in other rooms (with
more space than the room the studio occupies), I'll plug
my Røde NT2 into the Native Instruments Audio Kontrol
for portability. The Audio Kontrol is also great for laptop
DJing, and comes with some very cool bundled software.

Do you use samples, or pre-recorded beats?
Yes – I've built up a huge library of samples over the past
15 years. Propellerhead's Reload application moved the
library from old S3200 ZIP discs over to Reason NN19
sample format. I also use the SP1200's crunchy 12-bit
sampling for certain tracks. For sound sketches the
GarageBand JamPacks are incredibly useful – you hear
many of the motifs in film and TV use.

**Can you explain any unusual recording techniques you
have used to capture a particular sound?**
When I was working on tracks for *When It Hits You Feel
No Pain* I collaborated with an old friend, Dublin poet

Bennan Murphy. All of the spoken word performances were recorded on a portable DAT player in his kitchen in one evening, all one take, after a rather major bender the day before. I once played back a house track really loud, then recorded the sound from a microphone hanging out a first-floor window ... the results were interesting. Early on I made a drum kit with producer Adam Fuest from kicking some large flight cases and recording into an MPC 60 – the joys of sampling.

Do you use any unconventional instruments, or take samples from 'the world around you' to use in your music?
I recorded ambience, street/pub noises and environmental sounds in Dublin and Doolin during the same visit and added to a couple of the tracks.

Do you enjoy recording at home?
Yes – you can really get familiar with everything to do with your home studio, and get the most from your set-up. A big advantage is instant recall, so you don't lose your train of thought if you want to put down a new idea for something you're working on – you're recording your new idea in minutes.

Do you think musicians/producers can generate album-quality material at home, or is it better to use a studio?
It depends on the target market, in my opinion. Pop acts will be sonically competing with big-sounding

productions mixed on high-end SSL or Neve desks, so need to be hitting at the same level. Also, if one is after a vintage sound, you need vintage gear (e.g. Roth-Händle, Stockholm). Having said that, I think one can definitely produce release-quality material at home, but it's probably worth getting it mastered if it's to be a commercial release or you're looking for mainstream radio play.

Do you have a record/publishing deal?
Yes – with Seeca, a company set up by Louise Martins, who I've worked with for years. Louise and her team have built a really interesting roster of acts, and I'm happy to be their main sync person.

Can you give one or two recommendations to other people who are getting into recording music at home?
If you can afford it it's worth working on a Mac. Life for a Mac-based composer/producer/musician is just easier. I say this as someone who resisted moving from an Atari ST for some time. Many PC-based musicians I know, who eventually moved to Mac, all regret not having made the move sooner.

Also – try not to create in a vacuum. Once your tracks are ready, get them out there however you can; if they sit on the shelf there's just no point. Digital platforms such as MySpace, Last.fm and IndieStore.com make it easier than ever to distribute and sell your music online. Online music sites such as Video-C can help get you noticed in the crowd. If you hook up with a manager, publisher,

>>

lawyer, someone in the music business already, and they like what you do, they might be able to provide you with invaluable perspective, and can help you move quickly to where you want to be.

A favourite recording anecdote?

I was due to record some spoken word by Nell Murphy for a techno track I was working on. I met up with her brother, my old friend Bennan, earlier in the evening as he was visiting London. Bennan and myself attended the opening of a synth museum in London's Turnkey music shop – a live theremin performance by Robert Moog and free booze ... result: some hours later, and several sheets to the wind, Bennan and myself turn up at Nell's, portable DAT in hand, for the performance. While Nell was getting ready I got Bennan to read into the DAT for a soundcheck. He pulled out a battered-looking notepad and read out something he'd written on the eve of his thirtieth birthday while travelling in India, a 'Statement on the approach of an unimportant date'. The evening quickly disintegrated from that point on, but the soundcheck vocal ended up as the finished 'Credo', the closing track on the LP and a personal favourite.

Glossary

Here is a selection of some of the technical terms you might come across when reading about home recording. Many of the handbooks for the software and sequencer packages will mention these. While this is by no means comprehensive, it should help to give you a small insight into some of the basics.

AC: Alternating Current.

A/D [A-D] CONVERTER: Circuit for converting analogue waveforms into a series of equally spaced numerical values represented by binary numbers. The more 'bits' a converter has, the greater the resolution of the sampling process.

ALGORITHM: Computer program designed to perform a specific task. In the context of effects units, algorithms usually describe a software building block designed to create a specific effect or combination of effects.

ALIASING: When an analogue signal is sampled for conversion into a digital data stream, the sampling frequency must be at least twice that of the highest frequency component of the input signal. If this rule is disobeyed, the sampling process becomes ambiguous as there are insufficient points to define each cycle of the waveform, resulting in enharmonic frequencies being added to the audible signal.

AMBIENCE: The result of sound reflections in a confined space being added to the original sound. Ambience may also be created electronically by some digital reverb units. The main difference between ambience and reverberation is that ambience doesn't have the characteristic long delay time of reverberation – the reflections mainly give the sound a sense of space.

AMP: (Ampere) Unit of electrical current.

AMPLIFIER: Device that increases the level of an electrical signal.

ANALOGUE: Circuitry that uses a continually changing voltage or current to represent a signal. The origin of the term is that the electrical signal can be thought of as being 'analogous' to the original signal.

AUDIO FREQUENCY: Signals in the human audio range: nominally 20Hz to 20kHz.

AUX: Control on a mixing console designed to route a proportion of the channel signal to the effects or cue mix outputs.

BALANCE: This word has several meanings in recording. It may refer to the relative levels of the left and right channels of a stereo recording, or it may be used to describe the relative levels of the various instruments and voices within a mix.

BANDWIDTH: Means of specifying the range of frequencies passed by an electronic circuit such as an amplifier, mixer or filter. The frequency range is usually measured at the points where the level drops by 3dB relative to the maximum.

BOUNCING: Process of mixing two or more recorded tracks together and re-recording these onto another track.

BPM: Beats Per Minute.

BUFFER: Circuit designed to isolate the output of a source device from loading effects due to the input impedance of the destination device.

BYTE: Piece of digital data comprising eight bits.

CAPACITOR: Electrical component exhibiting capacitance. Capacitor microphones are often abbreviated to capacitors.

CAPACITOR MICROPHONE: Microphone that operates on the principle of measuring the change in electrical charge across a capacitor where one of the electrodes is a thin conductive membrane that flexes in response to sound pressure.

CD-R: Recordable type of Compact Disc that can only be recorded once – it cannot be erased and reused.

CD-R BURNER: Device capable of recording data onto blank CD-R discs.

CHANNEL: (1) A single strip of controls in a mixing console, relating to either a single input or a pair of main/monitor inputs. (2) In the context of MIDI, one of 16 possible data channels over which MIDI data may be sent. The organisation of data by channels means that up to 16 different MIDI instruments or parts may be addressed using a single cable.

CHORD: Three or more different musical notes played at the same time.

CLICK TRACK: Metronome pulse that assists musicians in playing in time.

CLIPPING: Severe form of distortion which occurs when a signal attempts to exceed the maximum level that a piece of equipment can handle.

COMPRESSOR: Device designed to reduce the dynamic range of audio signals by reducing the level of high signals or by increasing the level of low signals.

COMPUTER: Device for the storing and processing of digital data.

COPY PROTECTION: Method used by software manufacturers to prevent unauthorised copying.

CRASH: Slang term relating to malfunction of computer program.

DATA: Information stored and used by a computer.

DATA COMPRESSION: System used to reduce the amount of data needed to represent an audio signal, usually by discarding audio information that is being masked by more prominent sounds.

dB: deciBel. Unit used to express the relative levels of two electrical voltages, powers or sounds.

dBm: Variation on dB referenced to 0dB = 1mW into 600Ohms.

dBv: Variation on dB referenced to 0dB = 0.775 volts.

dBV: Variation on dB referenced to 0dB = 1 volt.

dB/Octave: Means of measuring the slope of a filter. The more dBs per octave, the sharper the filter slope.

DC: Direct Current.

DE-ESSER: Device for reducing the effect of sibilance in vocal signals.

DI: Short for Direct Inject, where a signal is plugged directly into an audio chain without the aid of a microphone.

DI BOX: Device for matching the signal level impedance of a source to a tape machine or mixer input.

DIGITAL: Electronic system which represents data and signals in the form of codes comprising 1s and 0s.

DIGITAL DELAY: Digital processor for generating delay and echo effects.

DIGITAL REVERB: Digital processor used for simulating reverberation.

DIN CONNECTOR: Consumer multipin signal connection format, also used for MIDI cabling. Various pin configurations are available.

DISC: Used to describe vinyl discs, CDs and MiniDiscs.

DISK: Abbreviation of Diskette, but now used to describe computer floppy, hard and removable disks.

DOLBY: Encode/decode tape noise reduction system that amplifies low-level, high-frequency signals during recording, then reverses this process during playback. There are several different Dolby systems in use: types B, C and S for domestic and semi-professional machines, and types A and SR for professional machines. Recordings made using one of these systems must also be replayed via the same system.

DOS: Disk Operating System. Part of the operating system of PC and PC-compatible computers.

DRIVER: Piece of software that handles communications between the main program and a hardware peripheral, such as a sound card, printer or scanner.

DUBBING: Adding further material to an existing recording. Also known as overdubbing.

DYNAMIC MICROPHONE: Type of microphone that works on the electric generator principle, where a diaphragm moves a coil of wire within a magnetic field.

DYNAMIC RANGE: The range in dB between the highest signal that can be handled by a piece of equipment and the level at which small signals disappear into the noise floor.

DYNAMICS: Way of describing the relative levels within a piece of music.

EFFECT: Device for treating an audio signal in order to change it in some creative way. Effects often involve the use of delay circuits, and include such treatments as reverb and echo.

EFFECTS LOOP: Connection system that allows an external signal processor to be connected into the audio chain.

EFFECTS RETURN: Additional mixer input designed to accommodate the output from an effects unit.

ELECTRET MICROPHONE: Type of capacitor microphone utilising a permanently charged capsule.

ENCODE/DECODE: System that requires a signal to be processed prior to recording, then that process reversed during playback.

ENHANCER: Device designed to brighten audio material using techniques such as dynamic equalisation, phase shifting and harmonic generation.

EQUALISER: Device for selectively cutting or boosting selected parts of the audio spectrum.

EXPANDER: Device designed to decrease the level of low-level signals and increase the level of high-level signals, thus increasing the dynamic range of the signal.

EXPANDER MODULE: Synthesiser with no keyboard, often rack mountable or in some other compact format.

FILE: Meaningful list of data stored in digital form. A Standard MIDI File is a specific type of file designed to allow sequence information to be interchanged between different types of sequencer.

FILTER: Electronic circuit designed to emphasise or attenuate a specific range of frequencies.

FLANGING: Modulated delay effect using feedback to create a dramatic, sweeping sound.

FORMAT: Procedure required to ready a computer disk for use. Formatting organises the disk's surface into a series of electronic pigeonholes into which data can be stored. Different computers often use different formatting systems.

FRAGMENTATION: Process by which the available space on a disk drive gets split up into small sections due to the storing and erasing of files.

FREQUENCY: Indication of how many cycles of a repetitive waveform occur in 1 second. A waveform which has a repetition cycle of once per second has a frequency of 1Hz (pronounced Hertz).

FREQUENCY RESPONSE: Measurement of the frequency range that can be handled by a specific piece of electrical equipment or loudspeaker.

FX: Effects.

GAIN: Amount by which a circuit amplifies a signal.

GENERAL MIDI: Addition to the basic MIDI spec to assure a minimum level of compatibility when playing back GM format song files. The specification covers type and program number of sounds, minimum levels of polyphony and multitimbrality, response to controller information and so on.

GLITCH: Describes an unwanted short-term corruption of a signal, or the unexplained, short-term malfunction of a piece of equipment. For example, an inexplicable click on a DAT tape would be termed a glitch.

GM RESET: A universal sysex command which activates the General MIDI mode on a GM instrument. The same command also sets all controllers to their default values and switches off any notes still playing by means of an All Notes Off message.

GRAPHIC EQUALISER: An equaliser whereby several narrow segments of the audio spectrum are controlled by individual cut/boost faders. The name comes about because the fader positions provide a graphic representation of the EQ curve.

HARD DISK: High-capacity computer storage device based on a rotating rigid disk with a magnetic coating onto which data may be recorded.

HARMONIC: High-frequency component of a complex waveform.

HARMONIC DISTORTION: Addition of harmonics that were not present in the original signal.

HEAD: Part of a tape machine or disk drive that reads and/or writes data to and from the storage media.

HEADROOM: Safety margin in dBs between the highest peak signal being passed by a piece of equipment and the absolute maximum level the equipment can handle.

HIGH PASS FILTER (HPF): Filter which attenuates frequencies below its cutoff frequency.

HISS: Noise caused by random electrical fluctuations.

HUM: Signal contamination caused by the addition of low frequencies, usually related to the mains power frequency.

Hz: Short for Hertz, the unit of frequency.

JACK: Commonly used audio connector. May be mono or stereo.

JARGON: Specialised words associated with a specialist subject.

k: Abbreviation for 1000 (kilo). Used as a prefix to other values to indicate magnitude.

kHz: 1000Hz.

LCD: Liquid Crystal Display.

LED: Light Emitting Diode. A form of solid state lamp.

LIMITER: Device that controls the gain of a signal so as to prevent it from ever exceeding a preset level. A limiter is essentially a fast-acting compressor with an infinite compression ratio.

LINEAR: Device where the output is a direct multiple of the input.

LINE LEVEL: Nominal signal level which is around -10dBV for semi-pro equipment and +4dBu for professional equipment.

LOAD: Electrical circuit that draws power from another circuit or power supply. Also describes reading data into a computer.

LOCAL ON/OFF: A function to allow the keyboard and sound generating section of a keyboard synthesiser to be used independently of each other.

LOGIC: Type of electronic circuitry used for processing binary signals comprising two discrete voltage levels.

LOOP: Circuit where the output is connected back to the input.

LOW FREQUENCY OSCILLATOR (LFO): Oscillator used as a modulation source, usually below 20Hz. The most common LFO waveshape is the sine wave, though there is often a choice of sine, square, triangular and sawtooth waveforms.

LOW PASS FILTER (LPF): Filter which attenuates frequencies above its cutoff frequency.

mA: milliamp or one thousandth of an amp. See Amp.

MB: Megabyte: 1,000,000 (one million) bytes of data.

MEG: Abbreviation for 1,000,000.

MEMORY: Computer's RAM memory used to store programs and data. This data is lost when the computer is switched off and so must be stored to disk or other suitable media.

MENU: List of choices presented by a computer program or a device with a display window.

MIC LEVEL: Low-level signal generated by a microphone. This must be amplified many times to increase it to line level.

MICROPROCESSOR: Specialised microchip at the heart of a computer. It is here that instructions are read and acted upon.

MIDI: Musical Instrument Digital Interface.

MIDI CONTROLLER: Term used to describe the physical interface by means of which the musician plays the MIDI synthesiser or other sound generator. Examples of controllers are keyboards, drum pads, wind synths and so on.

(STANDARD) MIDI FILE: Standard file format for storing song data recorded on a MIDI sequencer in such a way as to allow it to be read by other makes or models of MIDI sequencer.

MIXER: Device for combining two or more audio signals.

MONITOR: (1) Reference loudspeaker used for mixing. (2) Action of listening to a mix or a specific audio signal. (3) VDU display for a computer.

MONOPHONIC: One note at a time.

MOTHERBOARD: Main circuit board within a computer into which all the other components plug or connect.

MULTI-SAMPLE: Creation of several samples, each covering a limited musical range, the idea being to produce a more natural range of sounds across the range of the instrument being sampled. For example, a piano may need to be sampled every two or three semitones in order to sound convincing.

MULTITRACK: Recording device capable of recording several 'parallel' parts or tracks which may then be mixed or re-recorded independently.

NOISE REDUCTION: System for reducing analogue tape noise or for reducing the level of hiss present in a recording.

NOISE SHAPING: System for creating digital dither such that any added noise is shifted into those parts of the audio spectrum where the human ear is least sensitive.

NORMALISE: A socket is said to be normalised when it is wired so that the original signal path is maintained unless a plug is inserted into the socket. The most common examples of normalised connectors are the insert points on a mixing console.

OCTAVE: When a frequency or pitch is transposed up by one octave, its frequency is doubled.

OFF-LINE: Process carried out while a recording is not playing. For example, some computer-based processes have to be carried out off-line as the computer isn't fast enough to carry out the process in real time.

OHM: Unit of electrical resistance.

OMNI: Meaning all, refers to a microphone that is equally sensitive in all directions, or to the MIDI mode where data on all channels is recognised.

OSCILLATOR: Circuit designed to generate a periodic electrical waveform.

OVERDUB: To add another part to a multitrack recording or to replace one of the existing parts.

OVERLOAD: To exceed the operating capacity of an electronic or electrical circuit.

PARALLEL: Means of connecting two or more circuits so that their inputs are connected together and their outputs connected together.

PARAMETER: Variable value that affects some aspect of a device's performance.

PARAMETRIC EQ: Equaliser with separate controls for frequency, bandwidth and cut/boost.

PEAK: Maximum instantaneous level of a signal.

PHANTOM POWER: 48V DC supply for capacitor microphones, transmitted along the signal cores of a balanced mic cable.

PHASE: Timing difference between two electrical waveforms expressed in degrees, where 360 degrees corresponds to a delay of exactly one cycle.

PHASER: Effect that combines a signal with a phase-shifted version of itself to produce creative filtering effects. Most phasers are controlled by means of an LFO.

POST PRODUCTION: Work done to a stereo recording after mixing is complete.

POWER SUPPLY: Unit designed to convert mains electricity to the voltages necessary to power an electronic circuit or device.

PRESET: Effects unit or synth patch that cannot be altered by the user.

RAM: Abbreviation for Random Access Memory. This is a type of memory used by computers for the temporary storage of programs and data, and all data is lost when the power is turned off. For that reason, work needs to be saved to disk if it is not to be lost.

REAL TIME: An audio process that can be carried out as the signal is being recorded or played back. The opposite is off-line, where the signal is processed in non-real time.

REVERB: Acoustic ambience created by multiple reflections in a confined space.

RIBBON MICROPHONE: Microphone where the sound-capturing element is a thin metal ribbon suspended in a magnetic field. When sound causes the ribbon to vibrate, a small electrical current is generated within the ribbon.

SAMPLE: (1) process carried out by an A/D converter where the instantaneous amplitude of a signal is measured many times per second (44.1kHz in the case of CD). (2) Digitised sound used as a musical sound source in a sampler or additive synthesiser.

SAMPLE RATE: The number of times an A/D converter samples the incoming waveform each second.

SEQUENCER: Device for recording and replaying MIDI data, usually in a multitrack format, allowing complex compositions to be built up a part at a time.

SIGNAL: Electrical representation of input such as sound.

STANDARD MIDI FILE: A standard file format that allows MIDI files to be transferred between different sequencers and MIDI file players.

STEREO: Two-channel system feeding left and right loud-speakers.

SUB BASS: Frequencies below the range of typical monitor loud-speakers. Some define sub-bass as frequencies that can be felt rather than heard.

SYNC: A system for making two or more pieces of equipment run in synchronism with each other.

SYNTHESISER: Electronic musical instrument designed to create a wide range of sounds, both imitative and abstract.

TEMPO: Rate of the 'beat' of a piece of music, measured in beats per minute.

TIMBRE: Tonal 'colour' of a sound.

TRACK: Term dating back to multitrack tape where the tracks are physical stripes of recorded material, located side by side along the length of the tape.

TRACKING: System whereby one device follows another. Tracking is often discussed in the context of MIDI guitar synthesisers or controllers where the MIDI output attempts to track the pitch of the guitar strings.

USB: (Universal Serial Buss) High-speed serial communications protocol which allows (theoretically) up to 127 hot-swappable peripherals to be connected in daisy-chain fashion. USB devices can be unplugged/plugged in without having to reboot your computer. Popular on modern PCs and associated computer peripherals (printers, scanners etc.) but also adopted by Apple on their iMac and blue G3 machines onwards.

VALVE: Vacuum tube amplification component, also known as a tube.

VELOCITY: Rate at which a key is depressed. This may be used to control loudness (to simulate the response of instruments such as pianos) or other parameters on later synthesisers.

VIBRATO: Pitch modulation using an LFO to modulate a VCO.

VOCODER: Signal processor that imposes a changing spectral filter on a sound based on the frequency characteristics of a second sound. By taking the spectral content of a human voice and imposing it on a musical instrument, talking instrument effects can be created.

VOICE: Capacity of a synthesiser to play a single musical note. An instrument capable of playing 16 simultaneous notes is said to be a 16-voice instrument.

WAH PEDAL: Guitar effects device where a bandpass filter is varied in frequency by means of a pedal control.

WARMTH: Subjective term used to describe sound where the bass and low mid frequencies have depth and the high frequencies are smooth sounding rather than being aggressive or fatiguing. Warm sounding tube equipment may also exhibit some of the aspects of compression.

WATT: Unit of electrical power.

WAVEFORM: Graphic representation of the way in which a sound wave or electrical wave varies with time.

WHITE NOISE: Random signal with an energy distribution that produces the same amount of noise power per Hz.

WRITE: To save data to a digital storage medium, such as a hard drive.

XLR: Type of connector commonly used to carry balanced audio signals including the feeds from microphones.

Acknowledgements

In order to guarantee the accuracy of information, several online sources were used for research. I gratefully acknowledge the following:

Audacity (page 124–127)
www.guidesandtutorials.com/audacity-tutorial.html
© Guides and Tutorials 2007
audacity.sourceforge.net

Cubase (page 114–116)
www.steinberg.net/24_1.html
© Steinberg 2007

Fruity Loops (page 89–93)
www.flstudio.com
www.flstudio.com/documents/what.html
© FL Studio 2007

Garageband (page 48–50)
www.apple.com/ilife/garageband/
© 2007 Apple Computers Inc

Glossary (page 198–212)
www.soundonsound.com
© Sound on Sound 2007

Logic (page 76–84)
manuals.info.apple.com/en/LogicPro7_ReferenceManual.pdf
© 2004 Apple Computers Inc

Propellerhead Reason (page 110–113)
www.propellerheads.se
© 2007 Propellerhead, Sweden

Pro Tools (page 55–59, 61–70)
akmedia.digidesign.com/support/docs/M-Powered_Basics_
Guide_25680.pdf
© Digidesign 2005

Sony Sound Forge (page 103–107)
www.sonycreativesoftware.com/products/soundforgefamily.asp
© Sony 2007

Index